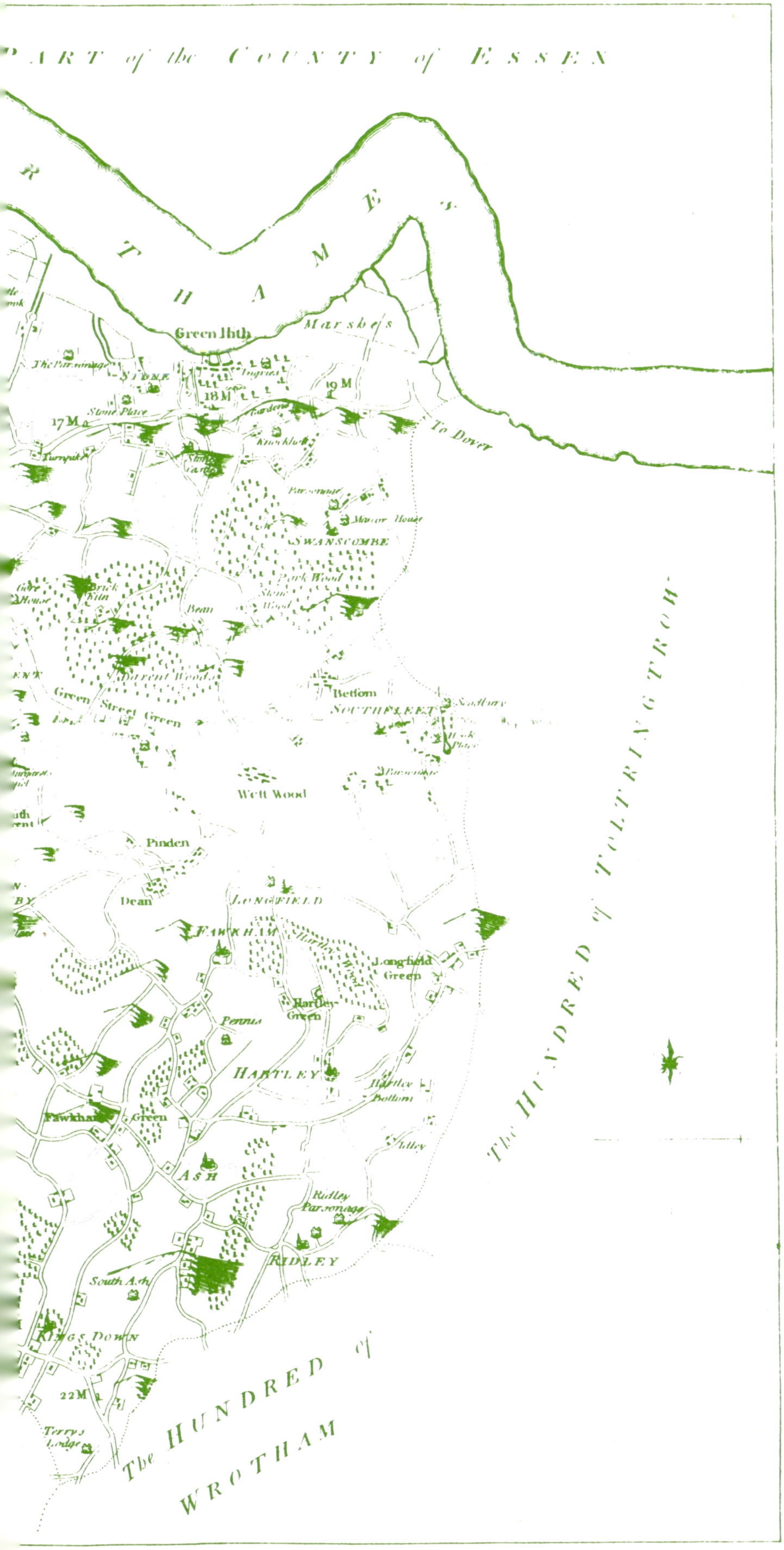
PART of the COUNTY of ESSEX
THAMES
Green Hith
Marshes
The Parsonage
STONE
Stone Place
Ingress
18 M
19 M
17 M
Knockle
To Dover
Swanscombe
Manor House
Park Wood
Bean
Darent Wood
Green Street Green
Bettom
SOUTHFLEET
Weft Wood
Pinden
Dean
LONGFIELD
FAWKHAM
Longfield Green
Hartley Green
Pennis
HARTLEY
Hartley Bottom
Fawkham Green
ASH
Ridley Parsonage
RIDLEY
South Ash
KINGS DOWN
22 M
Terrys Lodge
The HUNDRED of TOLTRINGTROW
The HUNDRED of WROTHAM

Dartford Country 1985
has been published
in a Limited Edition
of which this is

Number 783

A complete list of the
original subscribers
is printed at the
back of the book

DARTFORD COUNTRY

FRONT COVER: Stone Castle, (the seat of Robert Talbot, 1829). The tower is the oldest, (medieval) part. (Engraved by Mottram). (KCL DD)

The old farmhouse (1471), Dean Bottom, Horton Kirby. (DH)

DARTFORD COUNTRY

The Story of the
Hundred of Axstane

BY

GEOFF PORTEUS

BARRACUDA BOOKS LIMITED
BUCKINGHAM, ENGLAND
MCMLXXXV

PUBLISHED BY BARRACUDA BOOKS LIMITED
BUCKINGHAM, ENGLAND
AND PRINTED BY
BUSIPRINT LIMITED
BUCKINGHAM, ENGLAND

BOUND BY
J. W. BRAITHWAITE & SON LIMITED
WOLVERHAMPTON, ENGLAND

JACKET PRINTED BY
CHENEY & SON LIMITED
BANBURY, OXON

LITHOGRAPHY BY
SOUTH MIDLANDS LITHOPLATES LIMITED
LUTON, ENGLAND

DISPLAY SET IN BASKERVILLE
AND TEXT SET IN 10½/12pt BASKERVILLE BY
GRAHAM BURN TYPESETTING
LEIGHTON BUZZARD, BEDFORDSHIRE

ISBN 0 86023 203 4

Contents

Acknowledgements

For the third time, I am delighted to be able to thank a number of people for their assistance in penning and illustrating a book on this area. In the first place I must thank the staff of Dartford Central Library (under Ken Jarvis, Group Librarian) for continuing to provide such unstinting help – in providing facilities for subscribers, in the matter of certain photographic material, and in guiding me to appropriate reference material, and all with great friendliness. Dartford may be assured that the Library remains very loyal to the town.

The Borough Museum under Curator Peter Boreham has likewise been most helpful and often willing to break off from some official task to give assistance. Peter's assistant, Chris Baker, as Director of the Dartford District Archaeological Group, has also readily assisted in that capacity, especially regarding photographs.

Far beyond Axstane, the Kent County Archives Office staff under Nigel Yates has been especially helpful in allowing me freely (and trustingly) to examine the Tithe Maps and Awards of all the Axstane parishes, as well as other documents. Kent County Library, Springfield, too must be thanked, for hauling up those huge and cumbersome A.J. Dunkin scrapbooks – 20 volumes no less! – for my attention.

The sources of photographs are acknowledged briefly by reference beneath them, but I must thank all those who have so readily responded to my requests for such material – including those whose photographs I have not selected for inclusion (this just shows how much valuable material people possess which seldom sees the light of day). To Mike Jesson special thanks for spending so much time taking and developing photographs; and to Mrs Audrey Gillham and Dartford Central Library again, for permitting me to use the valuable E.C.Youens collection. The British Library, the British Museum (Natural History), and the Public Record Office should also be thanked for their services.

Artist Derek Hicks has given much thought and care again, in producing the frontispiece and another drawing, and is joined this time by Reg Hollick who, though he lives in Bexleyheath, is very fond of Dartford and its villages. Much of my time was saved by Miss Iris Morris, who prepared the index. But I am sure there must be someone I have overlooked; if so, it is unintentional and I hope they will accept my apologies.

Finally, I certainly do not forget the Publisher and the Subscribers; obviously, without their basic interest the book would not have got off the ground. I can only hope that the end has justified the means.

Dedication

For Horace J. Balls,
whose notes have contributed so much
to this study

Preface

by John Newman

The hundreds, ancient subdivisions of the county of Kent, survived, only lightly disguised, until local government reorganisation in 1974. They are one of the many signs of centuries-long continuities which still exert their influence throughout Britain today. Mr Porteus, after his two books on Dartford, has here adventured into its hinterland, the hundred of Axstane, and tells us of the generations who have inhabited the area from before the Roman period until the present day.

Axstane is a slice of Kent, near enough to London to feel the pull of the capital city, but distant enough to retain far-extending stretches of open country and hundreds of buildings which tell of pre-industrial settlement.

Traversed by two railways and four trunk roads, Axstane might seem the sort of area one passes through in order to reach somewhere more interesting. But Mr Porteus's chosen territory can boast much that is of high interest. For prehistory, Swanscombe Man is a celebrated name. Lullingstone is memorable for one of the best preserved Roman villas in the country. Eynsford's castle is an outstanding survivor of the earliest type of medieval castle employing masonry walls. Among churches, St Mary's, Stone, is one of Kent's best, an exquisite thirteenth-century fusion of noble architecture and lively sculpture. Aristocrats may have chosen not to live in these parts, but at Lullingstone the group of house, gatehouse and monument-filled church, provides a perfect picture of dynastic pride in a gentry family. Farningham, on the old Dover road, constitutes a handsome memorial to Georgian coaching days.

In the last two centuries, admittedly, the spread of industry along the Thames and greatly expanded residential development produced little to give particular visual pleasure until New Ash Green, that prototype commuter village, was started in the mid–1960s. Mr Porteus brings the story up to the present day, to what, with the closure of Thames-side cement-works in the early 1980s, we must learn to call the post-industrial age. His last chapter faces into the future. Whatever changes may come, the opportunity is given to each generation to enhance or impair its environment. The successes and failures of the past are written across the landscape, a challenge and a warning to us and our successors.

John Newman

Note: John Newman is the author of the Kent volumes in Pevsner's *The Buildings of England* series (Penguin Books).

Aspects of Axstane

'Now be we returned into Mesopotamia, for so me thinketh that this countrie lying between the rivers of Darent and Medway, may not inaptly be termed.'

William Lambarde, *A Perambulation of Kent*, 1576 (Written 1570).

'See! from the great metropolis they rush,
The industrious vulgar! They, like prudent bees
In Kent's wide garden roam, expert to crop
The flow'ry hop, and provident to work,
Ere winter numb their sunburnt hands, and winds
Engaol them, murmuring in their gloomy cells. . . '

Christopher Smart, *The Hop-garden*, c1740

'As the whole Shyre oweth to Swanscomb everlasting name, for the fruition of her auncient franchises obtained there. So I for the more honorable memorie of the place, can gladly afford it roome, both at the beginning, and toward the end of my labor.'

William Lambarde, *A Perambulation of Kent*, 1576 (Written 1570).

'After you leave Dartford the land becomes excellent. You come to a bottom of chalk, many feet from the surface, and when that is the case the land is seen to be good; no *wet* at bottom, no deep ditches, no water furrows necessary; sufficiently moist in dry weather, and no water lying about upon it in wet weather for any length of time. The chalk acts as a filtering-stone, not as a sieve, as gravel, not as a dish, like clay.'

William Cobbett, *Rural Rides*, 4 December 1821.

'Sutton for mutton,
Horton for beef,
South Darn for gingerbread,
Dartford for a thief.'

Doggerel quoted by Edward Cresy (Architect),
Memorandum relating to my tour round the Parish(Horton Kirby) 1857

(On the Darent Valley and Eynsford) '. . .the valley. . .famous for its health, its honesty and its happiness.' '. . . the people of the village are intelligent – and consequently polite – beyond their station in life.'

Pictorial Times, 1846.

'The hunters came in, and surrounded the spoil
A little the worse for the length of the toil;
For report it we credit, and most think we may
We had rode fifty miles thro' the whole of the day. . .'

'We parted in friendship, like brother with brother
And some they rode one way, and some went another;
Confessing such sport, with such marks of content
Was never before in the County of Kent.'

Verses (On a September hunt from Lullingstone to Cobham)
by The Man in Grey, 1830.

'The horses, the ploughmen with their slow motion, and the illfed labourer must give way to the mechanical contrivances of the age. The steam engines, the motive power, guided by intelligence must assist the labour of the field.'

Edward Cresy,*Memorandum relating to my tour round the Parish*, 1857.

'We hope that all this little scrap who see
May have the power to say as much as we,
For Parson Sandford is, we all declare,
As good a man as e'er will mount these stairs.
And our Churchwardens they are good likewise –
May we all meet in peace above the skies.'

John Stockley, Painter
Wm Turner, Carpenter
(1818)
(On a piece of paper nailed under the stairs of the pulpit, Farningham Church).

'In memory of William Pounds of this Parish who died Nov. 24th 1822 aged 99 years.' "Thou shalt rise up before the hoary head, and honour the face of the old man, and fear thy God." Lev. XIX, ver. 32.

(From an oak board by the lych gate, Farningham Church).

A mill near Dartford, by A.A.Glendenning

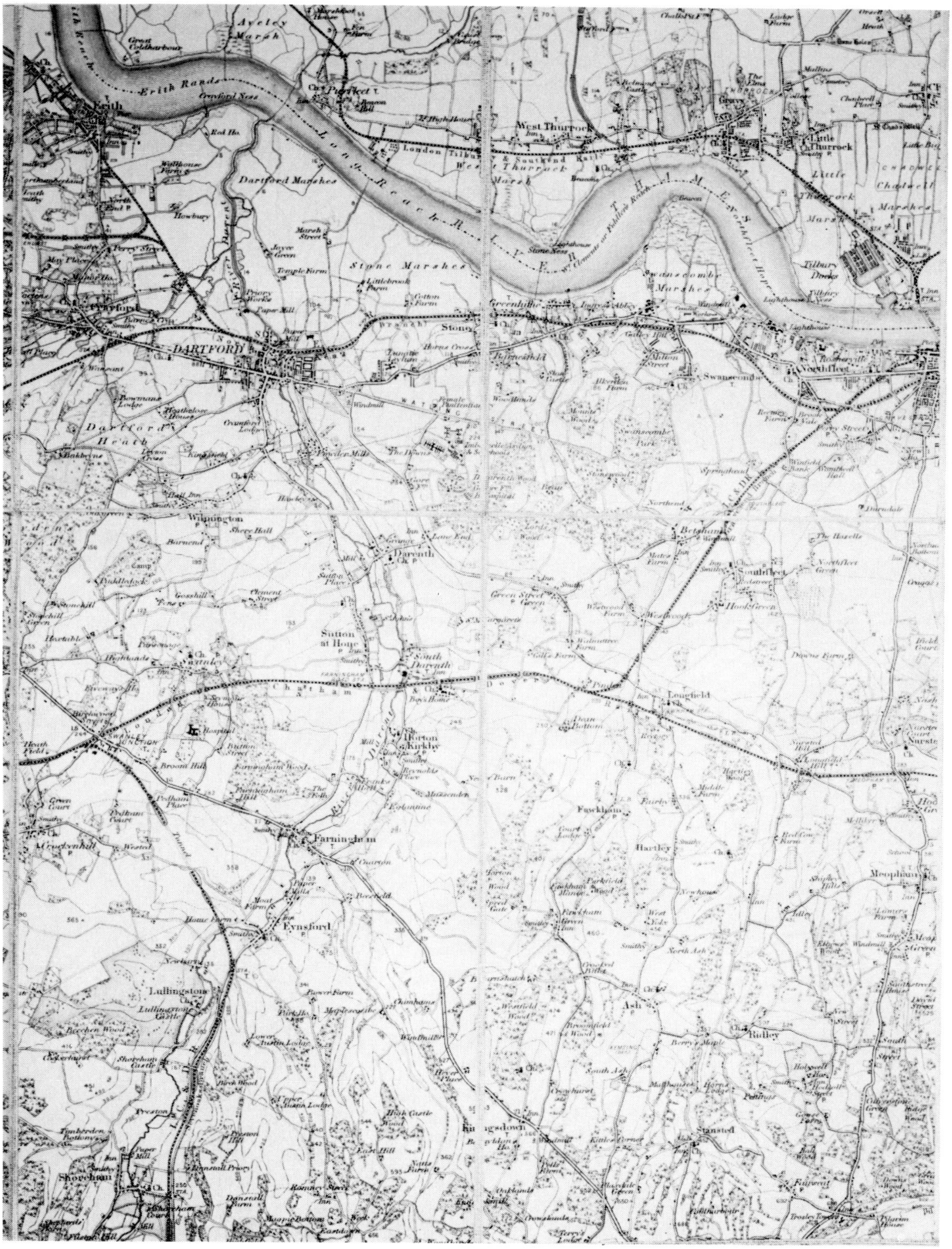

Map of Axstane Hundred, from OS map of 1869. (KCL, DD)

Purposes

The Kingdom of Kent was divided, probably in the 6th century, basically into seven Lathes. Some time after the Kingdom's absorption into Wessex, and probably in the 10th century, the Lathes were divided into Hundreds, areas possibly occupied by a hundred families (or ten tithings), or consisting of a hundred sulungs (a sulung was an area of land which could be cultivated by an eight-ox plough team).

This book endeavours to study the area of the Saxon Hundred of Axstane, one of the seven Hundreds in the original half-lathe of Sutton-at-Hone. Its name has been interpreted as referring to an oak-bearing stony land, but Wallenberg thought this unlikely and suggested that the prefix originated in a personal name, possibly Acca. The Hundred was later divided, part becoming the Hundred of Dartford and Wilmington, the remainder retaining the name Axstane. Dartford is excluded from this book, having been the subject of *The Book of Dartford* and *Yesterday's Town: Dartford*.

It is remarkable that the first (1933) Borough of Dartford and the former Dartford Rural District, together with Swanscombe/Greenhithe, covered virtually the same area as the original Axstane Hundred and, apart from the division mentioned above, and the later separation of Swanscombe, there was little change for over a thousand years in the overall area. More significant alteration came only with the local government changes of 1974, when the Rural District was split between the new Dartford and Sevenoaks Districts, the former being created a new Borough in 1977.

Since Saxon times there have been basically sixteen rural parishes in the Hundred (if we accept Lullingstone and Lullingst*a*ne as one, and that Wilmington and West Kingsdown – which originally had only chapels dependent upon Sutton-at-Hone – were separate entities). Although in modern times Sutton-at-Hone split into two with the growth of Swanley – first the village, then the town born of the railway a further mile distant; and Swanscombe also includes Greenhithe; while tiny, scattered Ridley has for long been linked with its larger neighbour in that antique description 'Ash-cum-Ridley' into which New Ash Green has recently been incorporated – the centuries' old layout essentially remains.

Much of the region's history, particularly in the north, has been influenced by Roman Watling Street (later the great Canterbury and Dover Road of pilgrim and Continental traveller) and less so by the other major highway, the Maidstone and Hythe road. Today they are represented by A2 and A20/M20. Overall has been the shadow of an ever-extending London, Cobbett's 'Great Wen' (a term more expressive of its burgeoning power), influencing both settlement and economy as well as communications. No stretch of land so situated could have avoided such influences.

I hope that this admittedly brief study will lead many to see the district with fresh insight, to see that it possesses varied scenery, villages and buildings (especially churches). In some sense it is a unique district, with manufacturing and extractive industries working closely beside agricultural areas; an ancient landscape cradling modern developments. Seen thus, this small area of only about 70 square miles is of intense fascination.

LEFT: The Swanscombe skull, from behind. (BM Nat Hist) RIGHT: Mammoth tusk, from Barnfield Pit, Swanscombe, 1935. (KCL DD) BELOW: Hulberry Neolithic (?) site 1917. (KCL DD)

Of the Earth, Earthy

What is this earth beneath Axstane Hundred?

For our purpose we may disregard the fundamental rocks far below of the Devonian period (about 350 million years old) and consider only those we recognise on the surface. The chalk for instance is the oldest, laid down about 100 million years ago beneath a moderately shallow sea. The ebb and flow of this great sea, together with the development of a vast river flowing from west to east to the north of our area, and the subsequent upfolding of the Wealden Dome, gave rise to the present geology and geography.

Long before the upfolding occurred, the loams, silts and sands known as the Thanet Sands were deposited over the chalk; lagoon conditions brought the Woolwich Beds and a returning sea brought the sands and smooth pebbles of the Blackheath Beds. With the shallowing of this sea came the London Clay. Mammals appeared, and the period closed about 45 million years ago. Millions of years later the great upthrusting of the Alps was reflected in the raising of these hitherto horizontal beds in the Wealden Dome, spanning the area from the northern river to the area now the English Channel. The drainage system which resulted included our own River Darent. Later still, weathering, the great Ice Ages (ending only about 10,000 years ago), and land subsidence wrought the changes which bring us to the present. Weathering reduced the height of the chalk (worn away entirely between the North and South Downs) and probably furthered the development of the clay-with-flints widely exposed in southern Axstane's fields, while close proximity to glaciation probably caused subsidence and formation of the many dry valleys. The great river, in shrinking to our Thames, left a series of gravel terraces, the most notable being the 100ft terrace of Boyn Hill gravel.

The result? To the south, on the North Downs south-east of a line drawn from Crockenhill to Southfleet, the chalk and clay-with-flints dominate, while in the valleys are flood-plain gravels. North-east of this line, now represented mainly by the higher ground of Joydens Wood and around Swanley, Swanley and Farningham Woods, and Darenth Woods and Swanscombe Park, are the remaining areas of Thanet Sands. These are topped west of the Darent Valley by the Woolwich and Blackheath Beds, and in the Darenth Wood-Swanscombe Park area by Woolwich Beds, London Clay and the much later Plateau Gravel. More significantly, overlying the Thanet Beds on Dartford Heath and Brent, and in isolated areas east to Swanscombe, are those famous Boyn Hill Gravels in which the remains and artefacts of early man have been found.

Long after man had arrived, geology and geography continued to evolve. Human and animal remains were covered by the gravels, the Coombe Rock (found in the Ebbsfleet Valley east of Swanscombe) and brickearths were deposited; and the great river shrank, while weathering broke up its terraces, thus isolating the occupation sites. About 8,000 years ago the Straits of Dover were cut and a more temperate climate developed. The Darent deposited flood-plain gravels and alluvium, while the Thames was the main contributor forming the Dartford, Stone and Swanscombe marshes. The discovery of human evidence reminds us that this present is not the final state of things. There are no eternal hills; we work, play, even lie, in an ever-changing landscape.

'One of the most famous archaeological sites in the world' and 'the richest Palaeolithic site in Britain' said J.G.Evans and J.Waechter respectively of Barnfield Pit, Swanscombe, where in 1935, 1936, and 1955 were found the three sections of the famous Swanscombe skull. The first discovery, by Alvan T. Marston (who also discovered the second section), has been commemorated by the unveiling by the celebrated broadcaster Magnus Magnusson, of a plaque in 1985, the 50th anniversary. The 1955 find was made by J.G.Wymer.

Swanscombe Man lived during the second Interglacial period, about 250,000 years ago and the importance lies much more in the fact that the skull represents an important stage in human development than proving early human existence in this area. This female skull represents a people living in open grassland beside a wide, gently flowing river, hunting and fishing for subsistence. There were both fierce and potentially domestic animals inhabiting the area, while remains of mammoth have beeen discovered on both sides of the Thames.

Flint flake tools and working sites of the first flint industry, the Clactonian, were found in lower (earlier) levels of gravel and loam at Rickson's Pit, Swanscombe, and in higher levels, flint core tools (hand axes) of the subsequent Acheulean industry, associated with Swanscombe Man. Slightly later hand axes were found at Bowman's Lodge and Wansunt Pit sites (Dartford Heath), at Wilmington, and in Dartford itself. Hand axes have also been found at Hextable, Hawley, Hartley, and implements at Warren Road, Wilmington. Flake tools of a later period (Levalloisian) were found at Baker's Hole (Ebbsfleet Valley) where the second oldest skull found in this area was discovered; this was probably of the Late Old, or Middle, Stone Age, like flint axes found at Darenth, New Ash Green, and near Terry's Lodge, near West Kingsdown. Activity continued in the Ebbsfleet Valley, where two working floors have been discovered.

Of the Neolithic period, when the first farmers appeared, few sites have been revealed, though occupation seems mainly to have been in northern Axstane, where the Ebbsfleet Valley again shows industrial evidence. Tools and hand axes have been found at Farningham, Horton Kirby, Sutton-at-Hone and Darenth, and tools and arrow-heads at New Ash Green. The Bronze Age is represented by a spearhead found south of Lullingstone Castle, and at Eynsford by a chisel and possibly by the sarsen standing stone (possibly a boundary marker) near the ford. Stone Court produced a spearhead and Swanscombe a decorated axe. Greater exploration seems to have occurred during this period, and Darent Valley finds appear to centre around Otford, where the Valley opens out into Holmesdale. A more strategically defensive basis for settlement may be perceived durng the Iron Age, culminating in the hillforts of Oldbury, Keston, Westerham (Squerryes) and possibly at Hulberry (Lullingstone Park). Other Iron Age occupation is represented at Marsh Field Pits and Goss Hill, Sutton-at-Hone, on Farningham Hill, in Lullingstone Park, and at Pinden. A pentagonal enclosure near Salt Farm (near the junction of Longfield, Fawkham and Horton Kirby parish boundaries) may be of this or the Roman period. But the largest site was probably that at Stone Castle Quarry, and consisted of two enclosures, the larger probably for cattle. Occupation here seems to have ceased with the Belgic invasion (1st century BC) but was apparently revived during Roman times.

The development of pastoral farming probably initiated settlement or tribal boundaries, especially in the Darent Valley. Certainly the Medway, boundary between East and West Kent, seems to have been recognised in prehistoric times. Belgic pottery and a cremation site have been found at Stone; at Eastwood Farm, Fawkham, another site may originally have been Belgic before being re-developed in the Romano-British period. Similar evidence was discovered beneath the Romano-British villa near Franks Hall, Horton Kirby. A cemetery at Stone continued in use during the Roman period. Lynchets at Farningham and in Lullingstone Park may have been of this period, though the latter site is open to alternative interpretations, possibly as a second hill-fort. Overall there is evidence of increasing settlement of the area which a new invasion was to accelerate.

Darenth Roman Villa, general view looking SW (1894 excavation). (ECY/
KCL DD)

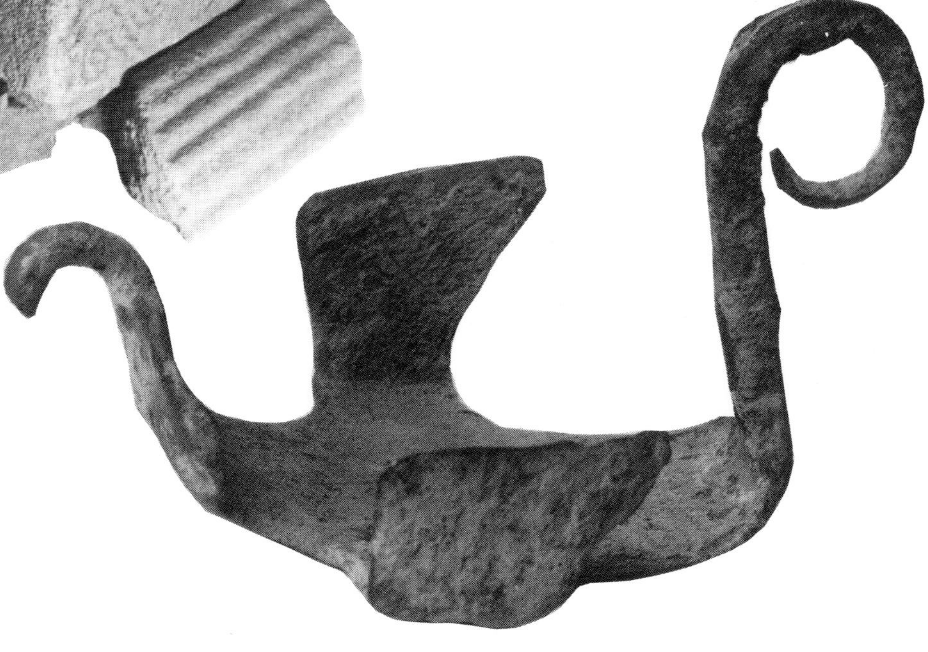

LEFT: Vagniacae (Springhead) Roman altar. (KCL DD) RIGHT: Darenth Roman Villa, hypocaust: Mr George Payne, FLS FSA in charge of excavation 1894, (ECY/KCL DD) and BELOW: Roman sandal. (KCL DD)

Roman Caesar to Norman Duke

A thousand years are encompassed by the Roman occupation and the ensuing Saxon settlement – longer than from the Norman Conquest to today. Julius Caesar's reconnaissance (55 and 54 BC) was followed in AD 43 by resolute invasion, and occupation continued for over a third of that thousand years (until about AD 410).

Since this area was on the direct line of the Roman advance (soon developed as Watling Street) and includes part of the fertile Darent Valley, it is small wonder that much evidence of Roman settlement has been found here. The military camp established at Springhead (*Vagniacae*) presaged a substantial settlement there, with workshops and eventually several temples. The Darent Valley has produced most evidence, with villas or other buldings at Dartford, Wilmington, Darenth, Horton Kirby, Farningham, Eynsford, Lullingstone, and (beyond Axtane) Shoreham and Otford. The most noteworthy sites were Darenth and Lullingstone, the former excavated in 1894–5 by George Payne FSA, the latter since World War II by Lt Col G.W.Meates FSA. The Darenth villa appears to have commanded a large agricultural estate, possibly of about 1,000 acres, probably for the production of grain; Lullingstone villa, with its mosaic floors and frescoed walls, was clearly a house of some luxury, possibly a Roman official's country residence. In addition to these buildings, there were also farm enclosures at Sutton, Farningham, and Lullingstone.

A significant increase in settlement seems to have taken place about AD 100. The reduction of the Oldbury Hill-fort probably led to increased confidence in more isolated settlement. Well-drained locations with easily turned soils were usually chosen, most of them – for these reasons – in the north of the area, and not far distant from Watling Street (*ie* Stone, Greenhithe, Galley Hill, Betsham, and Southfleet), but discoveries have also been made at Ash (with New Ash Green), Hartley, and Fawkham. The farmstead site at Eastwood Farm, near Fawkham Green was re-settled during the later 1st century; pottery and six bronze brooches were recovered. The Stone Castle Quarry hut-circles were re-occupied during the 1st to 3rd centuries, but only a small outbuilding with three ovens was discovered. The site is closely paralleled by a Joyden's Wood (Wilmington) 2nd century site, where again little real evidence of buildings has been traced. Near Stone Castle a Romano-British interment, with associated pottery and iron objects, was found. A kiln in Joyden's Wood may have been Roman, and tile-kilns have also been discovered at Swanscombe (Galley Hill), Springhead, Southfleet and Hartley.

At Ash two small villas have been excavated, at New Ash Green a ditched enclosure, at Southfleet an inhumation burial and – unusually – a milestone, and at Betsham a possible industrial hearth. Near Green Street Green are Roman foundations and across the shallow valley at Gill's Farm, are extensive ditches and banks. Foundations have been found in Horton and Farningham Woods and at Greenhithe, and signs of occupation on Swanscombe, Stone and Dartford marshes suggest pottery making, stock raising, or even sites for salt pans.

All this evidence points to enterprising and steady settlement of this newly pacified corner of south-east Britain. But even before the end of the 3rd century, Saxon sea-raiders threatened British shores, while the 4th century witnessed increased defensive operations under the Count of the Saxon Shore. Defence of Rome itself required the withdrawal of the army and, by about AD 410, the troops had left, and the Emperor Honorius advised the *civitates* of Britain to look to their own shields for defence. Symbolic was the burning of the Lullingstone Villa.

Some years later the Britons, under Vortigern, made an accord with the Saxons, by which the latter appear to have been allowed to occupy Thanet. Probably pressure by new settlers from the Rhineland, Frisia and Jutland forced Hengist and Horsa to thrust westwards. Battles took place at Aylesford and (traditionally in 457) at Crayford, and a defensive linear earthwork in Joyden's Wood (the Faesten Dyke) may have been connected with these events. The *Anglo-Saxon Chronicle* says that 'the British fled with great fear to London'. With them retired the British church leaders and the spread of Christianity was interrupted.

Fresh waves of settlers, from North Germany and of different stock, arrived, and new forms of settlement began – one of small villages, hamlets and scattered farms. Only one of Axstane's villages has been founded since Saxon times, and that in our own day (New Ash Green). The gradual development of a manorial system ensured little change in the settlement pattern over the centuries between. The principle of gavelkind (equal division of property among sons), retained in Kent, probably led at first to an increased number of outlying hamlets and farms but many, perhaps most, were established by 1066, when codification in the Domesday Record and the development of an even stricter feudal structure tended to perpetuate the existing pattern of settlement.

The village names are evidence of their Saxon (Jutish) origin, though Darenth which, like Dartford, derives its name from the river, may be even earlier. The interpretation of place names is a continuing study and is not so simple as may appear from the more obvious examples, such as Eynsford (*Aegen's Ford*). Thus, the suffix *tun* denoting a farm or settlement, continued to be appended to new settlements in the 13th century. It has been suggested by B.H.Cox that *ham* (homestead or village) may have been the first suffix form used by the Saxons, and that where *inga* precedes it, then transition to the Christian era (6th to 7th centuries) is indicated. Betsham and Farningham may bear out this theory, the latter – like Fawkham (*Fealcnaham*) – having a personal prefix. Wilmington (*Wighelm's Tun*), Sutton-at-Hone (south settlement at the boundary – presumably of the Royal Manor of Dartford), Horton (muddy farmstead – Kirby was a medieval personal name addition), and Lullingstone (*Lulling's Tun*) are four examples bearing the *tun* suffix. *Stane*, as in Stone or Lullingst*ane*, the early neighbour of Lullingstone, may refer to a boundary stone but by its similarity with *tun* indicates one of the difficulties involved in the study. Swanscombe was once *Suinescamp* (field for swine-feeding rather than 'Sweyn's Camp', an alternative often suggested); the same theme is suggested by Swanley (swine-herd's meadow). The suffix to Maplescombe also evolved from *camp* (*Mapledescamp* – possibly the field of maples) into *combe*, a valley. Kingsdown may have derived its name from Royal ownership, being closely associated, like Sutton and Wilmington, with Dartford. Southfleet (*Sudflete*) and Greenhithe clearly show their association with rivers, the former once lying at the head of the Ebbsfleet, the latter a small harbour or wharf on the Thames. Longfield (*Langafel*) may take its name from the narrow strip of land which forms the parish. Ash (*Eisse* in Domesday Book) is generally regarded as named from the tree, and possibly symbolic. The *ley* form in Hartley, Ridley and Hawley may suggest a clearing, with possibly a personal prefix. *Dens* are usually associated with swine pasturage in the Weald (much of it held by North Kent manors); local examples at Pinden (Longfield) and Alkerden (Swanscombe) may suggest a small valley.

In north-west Kent 37% of settlements are located beside rivers. 60% of settlements are on fertile, loam soils, while only 16% are on chalk and, while the former soils occupy only 29% of the soils area, the chalk occupies 45%. There were possibly 70 settlements in the 70 square miles of Axstane Hundred, the name of which suggests 'the stony areas associated with oaks'. Some of the villages – and farmsteads – may stand on sites adapted from Romano-British occupiers; evidence was found on the Lullingstone, Darenth and Wilmington villa sites. Thus around us is an antique and slowly evolving landscape.

With villages stemming from Saxon or earlier origins it is clear why Saxon evidence is so sparse. The wooden buildings have long since decayed, and even post-holes have long been built over. Documentary evidence is fragmentary too, so that only a sketchy indication can be made of the Saxon development. But the impressive cemeteries, particularly in the Darent Valley, show that the population was of significant numbers: at South Darenth nearly 100 graves were discovered when the London, Chatham and Dover Railway line was built about 1860; at Riseley, Horton Kirby, 112 graves were revealed in 1937–8, while at Eynsford 180 have been exposed. Material from Riseley, including swords, a sheild umbo, and a necklace of gold and silver pendants and amethyst beads, are now in Dartford Borough Museum. In one of several graves found near Darenth Park Hospital the famous inscribed glass Darenth Bowl (AD c450) was discovered in 1978; it bears the Christian *Chi-Ro* emblem. These discoveries relate to several centuries, from the 7th (Riseley) to the 10th (Eynsford). Single burials have also been found, as in Powdermill Lane, Wilmington, on the Stone-Dartford boundary, at Charton Farm, Farningham, and at Betsham. Other finds have included ornamental brooches, that at Darenth Park being of the late 6th century. During railway bulding at Lullingstone in 1860, a bronze bowl was found.

Gradually the 'Kentings' or *Cantwara* were welded into a kingdom, but the different racial stocks were reflected no doubt in the sometimes two kingdoms east and west of Medway. Probably during the 6th century the lathes (divisions of the kingdom or shire) were formed. King Ethelbert (560-616) is noted for his legal code; during his reign (597) Augustine came to Canterbury, and Christianity was re-introduced into Kent. The Diocese of Rochester was founded under Bishop Justus in 604. In the 7th century Wessex invaded Kent, but King Wihtred (695-725) stabilised the situation (and in 699 granted a charter freeing churches and monasteries from taxation). During the 8th century Offa of Mercia attacked Kent and soon after 760 Kent was annexed to that kingdom. Although Offa was defeated at Otford in 775 (with 'terrible slaughter', we are told) Mercia again dominated Kent from 805-25. How Axstane was affected by these dramatic events is not clear but, with its direct cross-country communications of Watling Street (called, in a charter of 814, *Casincgstraet*), and the Darent Valley, it would no doubt have echoed the general consternation. The Danes were a threat throughout the 9th century, over-running Sheppey in 832, attacking Rochester in 841, while in 885 King Alfred had to relieve Rochester and London from their depredations. In 894, they came up the Thames and Lea, and no doubt the Ebbsfleet, Darent and Cray experienced them; tradition tells that a nunnery founded by Ethelbert at Dartford suffered in a Danish raid and all the nuns were murdered.

But though suffering from the general turbulence, the Church began to contribute towards a growing stability. The ecclesiastical parish system was established, probably under Theodore of Tarsus, Archbishop of Canterbury, famed re-organiser of the Dioceses. Since the parishes were closely identified with the manors, with the lords often keen to found churches (and have a major influence on the appointment of the priest), this was often probably a two-pronged operation. The church buildings were probably initially of wood, later converted to stone. The *Textus Roffensis* of 1115 (believed to have been compiled from pre-Conquest material) records that not only Dartford possessed a church in late Saxon times, but Sutton, South Darenth, Horton, Farningham, Eynsford, Lullingstone (two), Stone, Swanscombe, Southfleet, Fawkham, Hartley, Ash, Ridley, with Wilmington, Hawley, St Margaret Helles (Darenth), and Maplescome having chapels. No doubt West Kingsdown and Longfield should have been included. Saxon work is still traceable at Wilmington, Darenth, Swanscombe, and possibly West Kingsdown.

About 975, the Bishop of Rochester, who was responsible for the first and third piers of Rochester bridge, ordered that Southfleet, Stone, Pinden (then in Horton) and Fawkham, all in Axstane, were required (with other manors) to maintain the third pier of the bridge. By the end of the 10th century the hundredal system was established.

Although Domesday Book was compiled 20 years after the Conquest, it contains much direct information as well as indirect guidance to the pre-Conquest position. The Saxon holders of manors are frequently named, the manor values in the time of Edward the Confessor are stated, and other manorial detail probably changed little during the intervening period. Despite certain omissions or lack of clarity a sensible, if somewhat fragmentary, glimpse may be attempted into the close of Saxon times.

The Royal Manor of Dartford was one of only four in Kent; the other three were Milton Regis, Faversham, and Aylesford. An oddity immediately presents itself, for the Dartford entry in Domesday includes Sutton-at-Hone which – despite its headship of the half-lathe – is not named. However, it was not unusual for the Saxons to have established their juridical and administrative centres a short distance from more populous towns. Since Sutton had ecclesiastical control over Wilmington and West Kingsdown chapels it becomes apparent that all three are included in the Dartford entry, and the three small churches mentioned may well be of these places. (While both Wilmington and West Kingsdown churches probably incorporate pre-Conquest material, Sutton was rebuilt in the 14th century). Certain lands in Sutton, part of the substantial Manor of Lewisham, had been left in 918 by Aelfrida, daughter of King Alfred, to the Abbot of Ghent, a tenancy-in-chief confirmed in Domesday Book. The lands may have included those which Osward, Sheriff of Kent under King Edward, leased to Alstan, Reeve of London. Hawley (*Hagelei*) has a separate entry, and was held by the Sheriff until his death, when it reverted to the King.

Darenth had been given by King Athelstan to Duke Eadulf, and in 940 was given to Christ Church, Canterbury. Accordingly, in Domesday Darenth appears in the long list of the Archbishop's Kentish manors. There were two mills, and five burgesses in Rochester contributed 6s 8d annually to this manor. There were two smaller manors in Darenth: one, held by Aelfric, was probably St Margaret Helles; the other, possibly Cleyndon, was held by Osgeard. Some land at Darenth together with land in Fawkham was left by Byrhtric of Meopham to the Priory of St Andrew, Rochester, during the 10th century. Beyond Darenth, Horton was originally one manor, but by 1086 had become four, three of which existed before 1066, and were held by Godel, Ording (from the King), and Alfward, who also held Ruxley and Otterden from King Edward. Godel's and Ording's manors each had a mill, while Alfward had half use of another mill, possibly shared with Farningham Manor. Farningham was divided into four manors. The largest was held of the Archbishop by one of his men-at-arms. Its pre-1066 value was £7, of which the monks of Canterbury had £4 for their clothing. The others were held by Brunesune, Dering and Alstan. Dering's manor had a mill, while Alstan presumably shared use of another with Alfward of Horton. Tiny Maplescombe had two entries, under Alstan (who held from King Edward) and Wulfstan (who held under one Harold). Values were £4 and £3.

Eynsford, with a value of £16, had belonged to the Archbishop since Dunstan's time and, like the main Farningham Manor, was held by a man-at-arms. There were two mills, and another mill and a fishery in Richard de Clare's territory near Tonbridge.

The southernmost of Axstane Hundred's parishes in the Darent Valley were Lullingst*a*ne and Lullingstone. Here were three manors, first those of Brixi Cilt (Young Brictsi) and Bruning, both held from the King. (Brixi Cilt also held Seal and Plumstead Manors). The third was held by Sewart Sot, a free man. Brixi Cilt's manor was based on the modern Lullingstone, the second possibly around Hulberry within the present Park, and the third at Lullingst*a*ne, where a chapel eventually stood close to the Roman villa site. The value of each manor was recorded as 60s. A mill stood at Lullingstane, the assessment for which was 15 shillings and 150 eels.

East now to Ridley and Ash: Ridley was held by Siward and valued at £3, Ash by Godric at £7, both held from King Edward. Godric may have been the same man who held seven other manors in Kent. One area is referred to as *Didele* (Idleigh) and another *Sonninges*, now a field name in

Horton Kirby, which may suggest a detached portion of Ash Manor. Alone of Axstane's manors Hartley (*Erclei*) was held by a woman. Its value was £3. Fawkham, Longfield, Southfleet and Stone were among lands of the Bishop of Rochester; Langanfelda (Domesday's *Langafel*) passed to the Bishop by a will of 964. Fawkham (*Fachesham*) had two mills, Stone (*Estanes*) a mill and a fishery. About 945, Littlebrook in Stone was held by Aelfstan's grandson Eadric, and was mentioned in a charter of King Ethelred, 995; values: Fawkham £7, Longfield 70s, Southfleet and Stone £11 each. Pinden was separately recorded and in 1086 was held of the Bishop of Bayeux. Before the Conquest it was held by a free man, Alfred, and valued at 16s.

Swanscombe, one of the larger Axstane manors, was valued at £20, the highest village value except for Darenth (£22). It had no mill, but possessed six fisheries and – probably at Greenhithe – a landing place. Finally there is unknown *Eddintone*, which Leofstan held from King Edward but after Leofstan's death went to Young Alnoth.

A significant aspect of many of these North Kent manors was that in Saxon times they held swine pastures – *dens* – in the Wealden forest, reached by drove roads. Although by 1086 many had been taken into Richard de Clare's Lowy of Tonbridge (the large area supporting Tonbridge Castle) Domesday Book still records them under their appropriate manors. All our villages except Longfield had Wealden dens. Darenth's Wealden land appears to have provided the very site of Tonbridge Castle. Lullingstone's dens were in Penshurst and Leigh, Sutton's in Penshurst, Horton's and Fawkham's in Leigh, Stone's in Hildenborough, Leigh and Edenbridge. In some cases (Ash, Ridley and Swanscombe) no pannage dues are shown, which may indicate that Richard de Clare had fully taken over their dens during this period of the system's decline and the beginning of Wealden clearance.

Domesday Book contains an interesting entry among its preliminary jurisdictional observations. Among those Saxons who are stated to have had full jurisdiction in the lathe of Sutton-at-Hone are Young Brictsi, Ording of Horton, Leofnoth of Sutton, and Edward of Stone, the first two of whom we have already met.

But the Book of Winchester (Domesday Book's formal title) primarily assesses the position from the Norman viewpoint. It categorises land ownership under the new order. For Kent (Chenth) under the heading 'Terra Regis' the first entry concerns the Royal Manor of Dartford, which included Sutton-at-Hone, Wilmington and West Kingsdown. After Hamo the Sheriff had acquired the Manor it was leased, apparently according to precedent, to the Reeve of London, a Frenchman. Hawley, being removed from the Manor, appears first in the summary of lands owned by Bishop Odo, who had inherited many of the Godwin estates. The tenant was Hugh de Port, though a Saxon (Wilfred) still retained 20 acres of the Hawley Manor, and acknowledged only the King as his lord. Many other manors in Axstane acknowledged the overlordship of the Bishop of Bayeux. Swanscombe was held by Helto, and answered for 10 *sulungs*, (the sulung was the unitary basis for tax assessment and was the amount of land which could be ploughed by an 8–ox team). Thus Swanscombe's 'land for 14 ploughs' may be calculated, at 200 acres to the *sulung*, as 2,800 acres, approximating to the parish area at the Tithe Assessment of 1843. Ralph, son of Thorold, held Hartley (and probably also, the unknown *Eddintone*, together with several other manors in West Kent. Ansgot of Rochester held one of the two Maplescombe manors; he also held Beckenham in Bromley Hundred, as well as several manors in East Kent. The other was held by Wadard, one of the Bishop's knights portrayed in the Bayeux Tapestry. He also held one of the Farningham manors, as well as several other manors and lands in East Kent. Ridley was held by Adam son of Hubert, who also held Otterden in Eyehorne Hundred. Hugh de Port, in addition to Hawley and many manors throughout Kent, also held Ash, where his man-at-arms had eight male and female slaves.

Brixi Cilt's Manor of Lullingstone came to Geoffrey de Rots, as also did the former's Manor of Seal. Geoffrey also held Otham, and a *yoke* (¼ *sulung*) in Newington. Lullingstane Manor fell to

Osbern Paisforiere, taking his surname in addition to its own; he too was an important landholder, mainly in East Kent. The third Lullingstone Manor – Siward Sot's – went to Mauger, who also held a Farningham manor and Pinden. Outside Axstane he held Ruxley and 3 *yokes* in Orpington.

The third Farningham manor was held by Arnulf of Hesdin, who also held Chelsfield, and Cliffe and Haven in Shamwell Hundred. Two manors in Darenth were held by Ansketel de Rots (or de Ros), whose main holding was at Horton, where he held the main manor and land in at least two of the other three. Known as the Marshal, he also held several manors in the Cray Valley and elsewhere in Kent of Bishop Odo and one *sulung* in the important Manor of Maidstone, as a man-at-arms of the Archbishop. The principal Manor of Darenth was held directly by the Archbishop. Two of his men-at-arms (Ansgot, and Ralph, son of Ospak or Unspac) held a manor in Farningham and that of Eynsford respectively. The Bishop of Rochester continued to hold Southfleet, Stone and Fawkham directly, but Longfield was held by Ansketel the Priest, a situation which led to the Archdeacon of Rochester having his residence as Longfield for centuries to come.

The King retained some land in several of the Bishop of Bayeux's manors, in several cases as 'new gifts from the Bishop'. Values had significantly increased, particularly at Southfleet (nearly double – £21), and Swanscombe (at £32, now the highest valued of the Axstane Village manors, up 60%).

An attempt at population assessment may hesitantly be made, assuming priests and slaves to be single persons, and others mentioned in Domesday Book to be householders with an average of four persons per family. Analysis on these lines gives figures reasonably proportional not only to stated manor values but (except for Darenth) also to the numbers of ploughs. The largest villages appear to have been Darenth (approximately 195 people), Eynsford (165), Swanscombe (160), Southfleet (155), with Stone close behind (at 135). Though this is necessarily a hazardous calculation it is interesting to compare the position at the first census (1801), when agriculture was still the predominant activity throughout the Hundred. Eynsford 841 people, Swanscombe (763) and Southfleet (508) now appear in the lead (in the same order as before), while Ash (472) has also overtaken Darenth (407) and Stone (403). Darenth's high position in 1086 may have been due to its relationship to the Archbishop, and to the close proximity of the Royal Manor and the London-Canterbury highway.

The population of the Hundred (excluding Dartford Manor) in 1086, estimated thus would have been 1,655; with Dartford, 2,255. In 1801, corresponding figures were 4,626; with Dartford and the former associated villages of Sutton, Wilmington and West Kingdown, 8,579. The heavier weighting of Dartford in 1801 may be ascribed to the town's increasing industries, and to the importance of its corn market.

At the close of the first thousand years since Caesar landed in Britain we now have a summary of the lands of Axstane Hundred: a number of small villages divided into one or more manors, many of which are represented by isolated farms still existing today. Around the village churches, mostly rebuilt in stone by 1086, were grouped the wattle and daub or timber-framed cottages, with the main tenant's (the lord's) home set especially close to the church. The water mills, if any, would obviously have been located by the village stream, the passage of which was most likely effected by a ford (even Dartford's bridge was not constructed until the 15th century). Around the villages were the arable and pasture lands so carefully catalogued in Domesday Book, with the woodland usually on the hillslopes above. Tracks linked village with village, with some convergence on Dartford and onto communal drove roads southwards to those distant Wealden dens. A basic structure had been established which has remained virtually unaltered over the ensuing 900 years.

ABOVE: Farningham Roman Villa, excavation 1925. LEFT: Watling Street, 1922, prior to building of first A2 (Darenth Wood on right), and RIGHT: 1924, after building of A2. (All ECY/KCL DD)

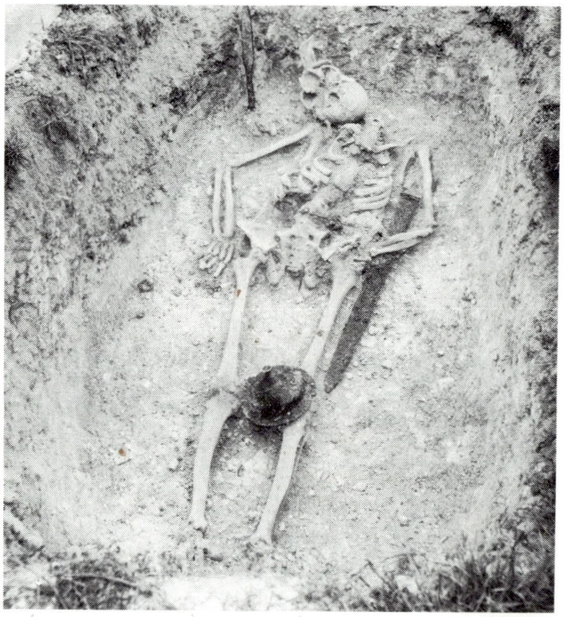

LEFT: The Darenth Bowl, 5th century glass. (RW/DDAG) RIGHT: Riseley, Horton Kirby; Saxon grave, with skeleton, shield umbo, and spear, (KCL DD) and BELOW: the Saxon cemetery excavation of 1938; (E. Greenfield, director, in foreground); 7th century. (CEF/KCL DD)

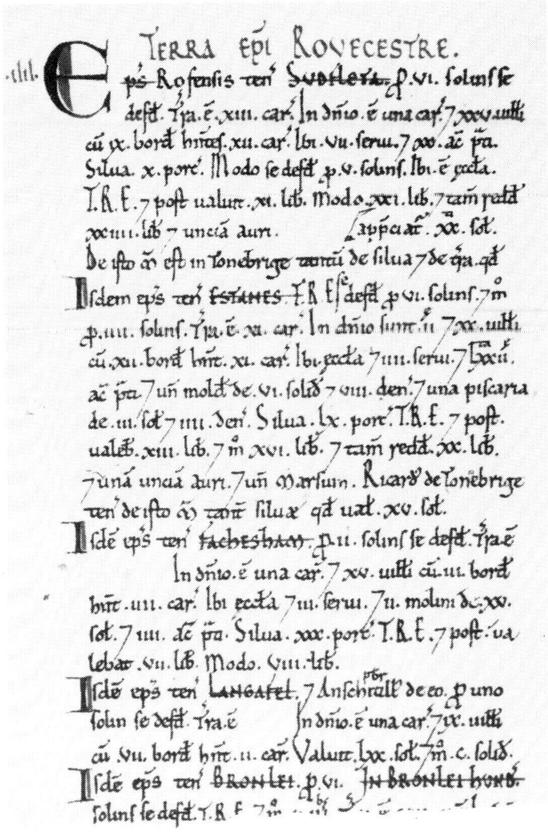

TERRA EPI ROVECESTRE.

LEFT: Swanscombe Church: pre-Conquest window with Roman tiles. (ECY/KCL DD) RIGHT: Domesday Book, 1086: Southfleet, Stone, Fawkham, and Longfield entries. (PRO) BELOW: Eynsford Castle (c1920), interior unexcavated. (KCL DD)

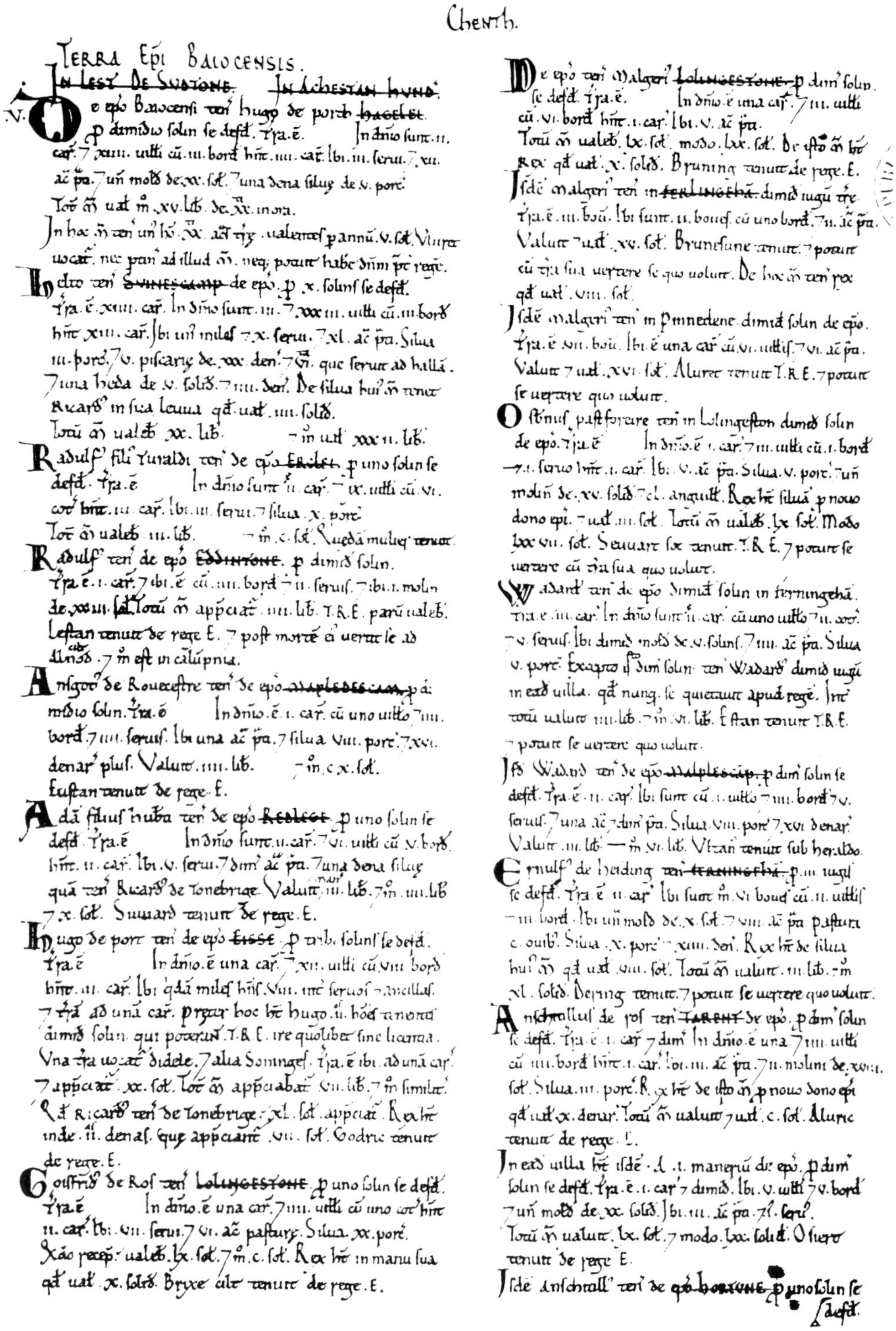

Domesday Book: Hawley, Swanscombe, Hartley, Eddintone (unknown), Maplescombe, Ridley, Ash, Lullingstone & Lullingstane, Farningham (part), Pinden, and Darenth entries. (Horton commences at foot). (PRO)

A Quiet Land

Within a district so close to London the nobility and Government officials often acquired the lordships of manors. The rise and fall of families, either for natural or political reasons, often effected change, as did inter-marriage. Occasionally manors directly connected become separated, and are eventually re-united.

As in Dartford there was a marked tendency for subsidiary manors to develop. Thus Wilmington had Rowhill, Stanhill and the Brockalls (Hook Green area); and in Swanscombe, Combes (Alkerden) became separated and Ingries (Ingress), long held by Dartford Priory, remains a separate estate today. Ash was divided into several manors by the 14th century: North Ash, South Ash (where the Hodsolls held sway), Scotgrove (now in Hartley), and Halywell (lands of the Benedictine monastery of Shoreditch). Stone soon evolved from its single manor, with Littlebrook and Cotton Manors and Stone Castle and Stone Place estates. Southfleet had the manors of Pole and Hook Place. Fawkham divided into two manors in Henry II's reign. By Tudor times the Manor of Horton was also divided into two, based on the 'Castle' (Court Lodge) and Kirby Court (Hall), while Franks and Reynold's Place were separate estates. In Eynsford, the first separation appears with the Manor of Orkesden (Aston, now Austin Lodge), and South Court, while eventually Little Mote and Petham Court became independent; the Crockenhill estate was held by Dartford Priory. One of Farningham's four manors, Charton, was divided into two. Kingsdown has a complicated, sometimes unclear, history. In the 13th century it was divided into North and South Courts, but in the late 14th century was re-united. (Earthworks in Church Wood associated with the manor house still exist). There were also the Manors of Hever (derived from the well-known Wealden family) and Chepsted. Maplescombe, a separate parish, continued with its two manors. Darenth's three Domesday manors seem to have remained virtually unchanged until 1713. There was however a celebrated exchange affecting Darenth in 1195, when the Archbishop, seeking a site for a palace near Westminster, exchanged his Darenth manor for the Bishop of Rochester's Lambeth. About 1190, another significant event affected Darenth, for evidence suggests that the Waldenses – refugees from religious persecution in Burgundy – were permitted to settle there. It is not known whether Sir Timothy Waldo (who owned Clock House, Green Street Green, in 1763) was descended from the original Waldo whose name the dissenters adopted.

Sutton (which then included Swanley) was held by several ecclesiastical authorities. The Knights of St John of Jerusalem (the Hospitallers) were granted the Manors of Sutton and Hawley in 1199 by Robert de Basing, and in 1279 a manor in Cowden was also granted them. When the Knights Templar were dissolved (1323) their lands in Dartford were settled on the Hospitallers, and Edward III made further grants. They also held the Manor of St John's, Ash. Much Swanley land was held by the Abbey of Ghent, (which held the Manor of Lewisham), Bermondsey Abbey, Dartford Priory, Cobham College, and the Knights themselves. There were thus no true manors in Swanley, only tenant farmers. Highlands and Gilden Hill, both ancient farmsteads, became the principal estates, although other farms developed. Hackstaple (Hextable) was a separate estate until 1876. Hawley had a second manor by the 14th century known as Haw Sawters.

There are two cases where adjacent manors became one. Gregory de Rokesley bought Lullingstone Ros in 1279 and in Edward III's reign gained a Maplescombe manor (and for a time held New Fawkham). John Peche acquired the de Rokesley property about 1361, and later Lullingstone Paisforiere. Mauger's Lullingstone manor seems already to have been absorbed. The two ecclesiastical parishes were united in 1412. Maplescombe's two manors were ultimately united by the Lovelace family's purchase about 1500.

Longfield became the traditional residence of the Archdeacon of Rochester. Longfield Court, a 14th century building close by the church, was unfortunately demolished in 1962.

There is no clear pattern of lordships within Axstane, but frequently manors were linked. Soon after 1086 the Montchensie family held Swanscombe and Hartley, a connection continuing until the 14th century, through inter-marriage with the Valence family (Aymer de Valence, Earl of Pembroke). After Aymer's murder (c1324) Hartley Manor was separated from Swanscombe.

During the 13th century Wilmington was held by Otho de Grandison and later by Sir John de Norwood, who also held Stone Castle, Stone Place and Littlebrook. In Wilmington Sir John was succeeded, in Richard II's reign, by Richard FitzAlan, Earl of Arundel, who also inherited Nicholas de Brembre's lands in Maplescombe. Thus five estates were linked. Nicholas de Brembre was more strongly connected elsewhere. In the 13th century Rowhill (Wilmington) and Highlands (Sutton) were held by Anselm de Gyse, who was succeeded by Simon Franceys (a Lord Mayor of London) and Nicholas de Brembre (who also held the Manor of Charles in Dartford). De Brembre was executed c1388, and Rowhill, Highlands and the Manor of Charles were granted to Adam Bamme, a goldsmith, twice Lord Mayor. This unity continued into the 15th century.

Three manors – Hever (Kingsdown), Orkesden (Eynsford), and de la Pole (Southfleet) were united during the 14th century under the prosperous Cobham family, who seem also to have had some connection with the Lullingstone estates.

During Edward III's reign 'Old' Fawkham was held by a later Otho de Grandison, and Ash by Sir Thomas de Grandison. Old Fawkham, with its manor house sited immediately east of the church, was later held by Sir Edward Poynings. The Percys of Northumberland also once held Old Fawkham, together with Ash.

In the 15th century Richard Nevill, Earl of Warwick, held Wilmington, the Manor of Dartford with Chislehurst (the two were closely linked until the early 17th century), and a Maplescombe estate. He was killed, however, at the Battle of Barnet (1471).

Thus there was a continual forging and breaking of links between some of the early manors. The ecclesiastical properties maintained a stability of ownership until the Dissolution. Dartford Priory held land in Wilmington (including Stanhill), Ingress in Swanscombe, Gilden Hill (Sutton), and the hamlet of Crockenhill, given c1471 by Sir Thomas Urswyck, a Yorkist and Chief Baron of the Exchequer. Bermondsey Abbey, in addition to its lands in Sutton, also held land in Farningham and Eynsford. Horton went by the marriage of Lora de Ros 'the lady of Horton' to Roger de Kirkby (from Lancashire) c1292, the marriage leading to the (modified) addition to the village name. In 1563 Horton was split when Thomas, Lord Wentworth, conveyed Horton Castle to Robert Rudston and Kirby Court to Thomas Walsingham.

The Sedley family was settled in Scadbury (Southfleet) by 1337. By the 16th century it held the Manors of Ridley, Hartley (and Northfleet). John Sedley (died c1530) was an Auditor of the Exchequer. The Swans of Hook Place, Southfleet acquired lands in Stone, Fawkham and Hartley and in Edward IV's reign, held the Manor of Combes (Alkerden). This family was much involved in official diplomacy and in 1404 William Swan attended the Roman Curia. He was a faithful follower of Pope Gregory XII during the Great Schism (1378-1417) and attended the Council of

Constance. A letter to him there by his wife Joanne was written at Hook Place. In 1555 Thomas Swan was pardoned, probably for being connected with Wyatt's Rebellion.

John Urban of Southfleet (died 1420) held lands in Southfleet and Fawkham, and also acquired the Manors of Hever (Kingsdown), and Hartley. The Black Lion, Red Street, may once have been a tithe barn, and in 'a street called Westwood.', (1417) there has for long been another thatched public house. The earthworks at Court Wood, near New Barn, apparently formed a medieval enclosure for livestock.

The Archbishop's Eynsford Manor had continued into the 13th century under descendants of Ralph, son of Unspac, and several successive Williams of Eynsford; then followed the Criols, the Zouches, and Chaworths, before the Harts added the manor to their Lullingstone estates in Henry VII's reign. In Henry VIII's reign they acquired the Manor of South Court, Eynsford, originally part of the Archbishop's estates. (During the 18th century Little Mote also went to the Harts, and later their successors, the Dykes, acquired Orkesden).

The Lovelaces were rising through society during the 15th century. Before 1450 they had acquired Hever in Kingsdown,and soon after that, land in Maplescombe, Ash and Dartford. In 1546 they acquired Woodlands which, during the 13th and 14th centuries had been in de Yaldham hands, and in the 15th century was held by the St Clere family. Although Woodland (Watlande in the *Textus Roffensis*) was originally in Codsheath Hundred, and in about 1570 the ecclesiastical parish was united with Wrotham, it eventually became part of Kingsdown for civil purposes. Later, the Lovelaces acquired Chepsted, and thus held nearly all Kingsdown and Maplescombe. They also bought Combes (Alkerden) in Swanscombe from the Swan family.

Early in the 16th century, Sir John Wiltshire (Comptroller of Calais, 1502–19) exchanged his land in Swanley for the Killingworths' manor of Cotton in Stone, where he already held Stone Place. Much of Sir John's correspondence with Henry VIII still exists; his monument stands in Stone Church.

Some manors have decayed. South and North Acholt, referred to in 1203, were probably to the west of Sutton and Wilmington; a medieval building foundation in Joyden's Wood may relate to Acholt. At Scotgrove occupation probably ceased soon after the Black Death (1348).

The turbulence of Henry VIII's reign led to many changes in land tenure, especially concerning lands formerly held by ecclesiastical bodies. In 1544 an important Government official, Sir Maurice Denys, Receiver General of the Hospital of St John, purchased (among other properties) the manor of Sutton-at-Hone and the Commandery buildings, for £536 14s, and also the lands at Ash. He then married the widow of the leaseholder of Brook (later Sutton) Place, Nicholas Statham. He also acquired East and West Brockall, Wilmington. Later, the Sutton estates were again separated, St John's going to his grand-daughter Martha Randall (who married Thomas Cranfield) and Sutton Place to her sister Catherine, who married Robert Wrote and founded the Elizabethan almshouses. (In 1780 the two moities were re-united under John Mumford). Wilmington Manor and Highlands (Sutton) went to Sir Thomas Moyle, Chancellor of the Court of Augmentations, which administered seized monastic property; later he became Speaker of the House of Commons. He eventually purchased the Eastwell estate, near Ashford. His monument, formerly in Eastwell church (now a ruin), stands in the Victoria and Albert Museum.

Dartford Priory's holdings at Gilden Hill and Crockenhill were eventually added to the Harts' Lullingstone estates. Stanhill went to the Dean and Chapter of Rochester, while John Beer – who in 1541 bought Horsman's Place in Dartford – acquired many of the Priory's lands in Wilmington and Ingress in Swanscombe.

The Bermondsey Abbey lands at Gilden Hill were held in 1546 by Dennis Topps. He alienated them to John Sybill of Leigh, whose daughter, last of the Sybills of Eynsford, carried them in marriage to the Bosviles.

Halywell or Holywell in Ash reverted to the Crown at the Dissolution and was then granted to Sir Martin Bowes. The Manor of Ash was held for a short time by Thomas Cromwell; on his demise it reverted to the Crown and was also granted to Sir Martin, whose son Thomas bought the Manor of Kingsdown in 1546 before selling it to Thomas Lovelace.

The Cobham College property in Swanley also came into private hands; one later owner was Joseph Hornsby, steward of the Cobham Hall estate, who built Kirby Court (probably the Hall) at Horton Kirby in 1738.

In Darenth, the former Archbishop's Manor which, after the Lambeth exchange, had been granted to the Priory of Rochester, was now granted to the newly established Dean and Chapter who, until the 19th century, installed tenants.

For his service in peace and war to Henry VIII Sir George Blagge was granted several properties in and around Dartford, part of the lands of the Stampit Chantry (Dartford Parish Church). Some land was in Darenth, where he had already inherited the Manor of Cleyndon, which his father had bought from John Crepehege. He held other property in Wilmington and Sutton. Sir George had accompanied Sir Thomas Wyatt on an embassy to the Emperor Charles V; later he was condemned to death for heresy, but was saved by Henry VIII's intervention. He later received his knighthood from Lord Protector Somerset. In 1582 Cleyndon was sold and by 1600 was held by the Filmers.

Lancelot Bathurst acquired the Franks and Highlands estates early in Elizabeth I's reign, together with a moiety of Charton in Farningham, all then following the same ownership descent.

This limited general survey may give some indication of the movement of land ownership from the nobility to court officials and professional men. Yeomen remained important, however. During the early medieval period, much partitioning took place, mainly through the Kentish system of gavelkind, though sub-division also began with the leasing of demesne fields for particular crops. By Henry VIII's reign the demesne of Sutton Manor was held entirely in severalty. But gavelkind also facilitated the growth of larger holdings through purchase or gift by relatives.

During the medieval period, demesne farming service carried out by villagers was overtaken by a system of paid labour. In Kent the medieval serf was little in evidence. Later the Black Death, the 100 Years War with France and the Wars of the Roses weakened the tie between workman and lord. Unemployment and vagabondage, and the attraction of growing industrial employment in towns, all accelerated the breakdown of the feudal system. One result was an increase in sheep-farming: a chapel to St Blaise, patron saint of woolcombers, was in Ash Church. By the late 15th century holdings had generally become larger and more compact. The commercial influence of the nearby and growing London market was already evident.

A landscape of fields of varying shape and size had developed; due in part to the Kentish turn-wrest plough, long-strip cultivation was absent. There were extensive woodlands as background to the villages, hamlets and isolated farms. Church and manor house were set close together, as at Darenth, Horton Kirby, Ash, Ridley, Southfleet, Stone and Swanscombe, to form the village nucleus; Southfleet in particular retains that character today. With Church and State in close harmony within the Manor, this was an almost natural development. Courts Leet and/or Baron are recorded for most of the Axstane village manors. The Sheriff toured the County twice yearly, although he generally attended only on the Lathes – in the case of Sutton-at-Hone, possibly at Shire Hall. The responsibility of this overall administration was for the raising of aids and subsidies for the Militia. However, the Lathe Courts gradually became anomalous, placed as they were between the manorial and hundredal courts on the one hand, and the Justices and Deputy Lieutenants of the County on the other.

To Farningham, on the Maidstone and Dartford-Sevenoaks roads, Henry III granted a four-day market charter to be held at St Peterstide. From Richard I, Southfleet secured a fair, and even St Margaret Helles in Darenth held a fair (on 20 July, St Margaret's Day).

The major crops were wheat, oats, and barley – with wheat predominating. Peas were also grown substantially. In Wilmington Neapfield may indicate turnips (neaps), while Lints suggests flax. Ploughing was by oxen, the main beast of burden.

On the Downs, chalk was much used for marling the soil, and in Wilmington, Stone and Swanscombe many 13th century dene-holes have been revealed. In some areas (Joyden's Wood) there were so many that it is accepted that chalk was also used for building purposes and for lime-burning. At least 13 shafts were discovered by J.L. Caiger, an authority on dene-holes, in Darenth Wood. They were associated with earthworks which suggest that the area was used as a private park for game and livestock.

Several villages possessed vineyards. Horton Kirby's modern school is sited on one; Wilmington's lay between Common and Broad Lanes; others were in Sutton and Ash. A vintner held land in Southfleet in 1466.

Hops appeared in the 16th century, and even today there are hop-gardens within 3½ miles of Dartford, at Horton Kirby. Before the end of Elizabethan times, the county was famous for its fruit. In west Kent bee-keeping was well known, and bee- boles (hive recesses) were built into walls, as at Scadbury Manor, Southfleet, at Eynsford, and in Farningham. Pigeons were kept for food, and the celebrated late 16th century columbarium at Hawley Manor, recently restored, has 549 nesting holes; a smaller, cylindrical one at Horton Kirby has 327. 'Pigeon House Field' in Darenth and 'Pigeon House Orchard' in Swanscombe, betray other sites.

The church was of course very much a part of medieval village life. The incumbent often held glebe land, the rent for which went towards his stipend: the rector particularly was entitled to his tithe in kind (or, in the case of a vicar, to his portion). If there was a Paschalfield – in Wilmington Paschalterfield *(sic)* – the income from this went towards providing the great Paschal candle for Easter Eve. Churchyard yew-trees were ordered to be planted by Edward I for protection of the church against storms; they also provided wood for archery bows. Their venerability led them to be regarded as emblems of immortality; that at Wilmington was transplanted from Calves Stock, Horton Kirby, in 1732.

Many of those whose story we read (and many less prominent) were baptised in fonts still regularly used, like the great sculptured Romanesque example (c1140) at Darenth; the plain but possibly even older one at Wilmington; the sadly worn chalk bowl at Swanscombe; or the two graceful 15th century examples at Farningham and Southfleet. Those many lived not far from the churches we see and admire, and may rest close by, the medieval graves unmarked unless within the building. In their wills they expressed wishes to be buried in particular places. At Kingsdown in 1451 John Medehurst requested burial in the *porticum* (the porch); Elizabeth Clement (Swanscombe, 1523) made a similar request, and George Clement, probably her husband, requested burial at the south door. At Southfleet in 1471 William Beare asked to be buried 'By fore the palme crosse', and another request suggests that this meant the churchyard cross.

Memorials within the church were simple tomb-slabs or, for the more wealthy, brasses or ornate monuments. Immediately inside the 14th century door at Southfleet a mutilated slab suggests a similar wish to that of Gilbert Carleton, Vicar of Farningham, in 1500, who requested that if he could not be buried before the high altar 'beneath the feet of the mass-priest' then 'under the step at the entrance to the church, so that every creature comyng in may trede upon my buriall'. A Fawkham 13th century wall tablet probably relates to William de Fawkham, who founded a chantry in 1274. Another at Southfleet may commemorate an important Rector, Thomas de Alkham (Rector 1323–46), who built the Old Rectory (now 'The Friary') and became Chancellor of the Diocese. Memorial brasses were long popular. At Lullingstone, John de

Rokesley, Lord of the Manor, is so commemorated (1361); another, a fine work of 1487, is to Sir William Peche, whose family succeeded to the lordship. (The date, most unusually, is given in Arabic numerals).

Several brasses recall incumbents, such as William Gylborne's at Farningham (1451), and half-figures, vestment-clad – John Tubney at Southfleet (1457), formerly Rector of Stone, Chaplain to the Bishop, possibly Chancellor of the Diocese, and Archdeacon of St Asaph, and Richard Galon at Ash (1465). But the earliest, and perhaps the most attractive of all Axstane's brasses, is that to John Lambarde at Stone (1408) with its small figure set within an octofoil containing a religious text. Among lay figures, John Urban of Southfleet is portrayed in brass with his wife, who died six years earlier, in 1414, when John provided a separate brass in her memory showing her in a graceful gown, with a small dog at her feet. Horton Kirby has the un-named brass to Alice Drayton (1461), daughter and heiress of John de Kir(k)by, while Darenth has that of John Crepehege and his wife Joan (late 15th century). Thomas Crepehege held the Manor of Cleyndon in 1483 and the family continued in Darenth for 200 years. In the 16th century, Southfleet had Thomas Cowell (1520) a small figure in a shroud, John Sedley, King's Auditor (c1520) and his wife, with two groups of children, and his grandson John (1581) and his wife Anne, (a Culpeper). At Farningham three people were commemorated by memorial brasses within five years: Alys Taillor (1514), William Petham, of Petham Court (1517), and Thomas Sibill and his wife (1519), presumably related to the Little Mote, Eynsford, family.

Stained glass early began to take on a more secular aspect, with heraldic shields commemorating important families. At Fawkham, the de Fawkham coat of arms may be 13th century, while Kingsdown's 14th century fragments may have heraldic significance.

Devotion was also expressed in benefactions, often briefly described on large display boards. In 1344 John Lucas granted land in Greenhithe for a chapel to the Blessed Virgin; this became the well-known Chantry. Many parishioners made bequests to their priest, and in 1445 the Rector of Southfleet was the beneficiary of the will of Charles Swan. In 1465 John Donett, godfather of William Sybyle (Sybill) of Eynsford left William 8 marks if he took the priesthood, together with 6s 8d for a new cope. In 1527 Sir John Wiltshire ordered 'a chasuble and tonycle with the albes, amyces, slotes... for a priest and his deacon to singe or say Masse in the sum of ten pounds', and John Launce, who was to be buried in the St Blaise chapel in Ash church, left 33s 4d for repairs to the church and £6 13s 4d for one year for an 'honest secular [chantry] priest'. John Urban ordered an antiphon(al) for Southfleet church in 1420. There might also be a gift from a priest to a lay person, as when Gilbert Carleton, Vicar of Farningham, left 'to my lady Pecche my book of Legende Aurea'. 'My lady Pecche' was presumably the wife of Sir John Peche of Lullingstone. In 1502 John Sibbill (sic) of Little Mote left money for lights in the chapel of St John Baptist (Eynsford church), in 1508 William Clerk left 'to the altar 40s' and in 1528 Nicholas Gybsonne *alias* Taillour, money for 'lights for the chapel of St Kateryn'. Edmund Finch, yeoman of Sutton, contributed to the 'Ester Feast 6s 8d'.

Church furnishings were not overlooked. Thomas Crippes at Hartley in 1527 felt the church required a new cross, 'of copper and gilt'; in Swanscombe, 1537, Richard Grope left for 'Payntyng of the clothe of the roode lofte...7d'. Although after the Reformation, it was perhaps inevitable that gifts for ritualistic objects should fall, bequests for maintenance of church building, a never ending need, continued.

Sustenance for the living was not forgotten by Simon Profest (Sutton, 1519), who willed funds for 'baken ii bushels of wheat and iii bushels of malt to be bruyd... to refresh such people as cum to the church... to preye for the helth of my soul and all Xten', or by Margaret Pye (1529) who authorised 'on barell of bere to be disposed of a monge poor people at my buriall'. At Eynsford Thomas Polly gave for 'keeping and norishing of a young childe.. founde in the chirche porche....iijs.iiijd' A bequest of John Beer of Dartford and Ingress in 1584 founded three almshouses in Greenhithe.

The registers of Eynsford commenced at a early date – 1538. There was no official census before 1801, but some guide to 16th century population may be approximately calculated working back from the Hearth Tax Returns of 1664 and 1671 and the Compton Census, an ecclesiastical enquiry of 1676 into conformity and non-conformity (including 'papistry'). In 1664 Darenth, Eynsford and Farningham populations were 257, 360 and 149 respectively (Dartford about 1,200). Assuming that the historian Chalklin is correct that from about 1550 to 1600 the increase was about 15-20% and that 17th century population remained stable, this would give (for 1550) figures of about 210, 300 and 120 for the three villages (Dartford about 1,000). Occupations, apart from the purely agricultural, included those of miller, wheelwright, cooper, carpenter, smith, shoemaker, fletcher, butcher, maltster, innkeeper, and carter. Some trades were often combined. At that time families averaged 4–5 persons, and infant mortality was high. Cramped living conditions, lack of sanitation or fresh water supply negated the effect of country air and contributed to the high death rate from tuberculosis, smallpox and influenza.

Some medieval houses, usually of the larger yeoman type, remain today. Wattle and daub buildings were gradually superseded. The yeoman type of hall-house, though heavily restored or altered, remain at Southfleet (Dean and Chapter farmhouse and the Church Houses), Wilmington (Lower Barn End Farm), and West Kingsdon (Crowhurst Farm), and in Eynsford. Court Lodge, Fawkham incorporates a 14th century aisled hall-house, while Scudders in the same parish is a timber-framed building with later, probably 17th century, plaster decoration of the front. Other timber-framed buildings remain at Dean Bottom, in a remote corner of Horton Kirby parish, but sadly yet more – in Sutton, Darenth and elsewhere — have been demolished in the 20th century. Longfield Court was a singular loss. Here, although the hall was much reduced in size, a late medieval roof remained, and the west range was stone-built. Southfleet's flint-built Old Rectory of 14th century Thomas de Alkham, though drastically altered, had an open hall and cross wings with solar; a mutilated crown-post roof remains. Much use was made of flint for houses and walls and much evidence remains, while many buildings have structural secrets hidden by later alterations. Barns remain in most villages and, if not wholly of original material, at least their earlier shape remains.

In Tudor times brick-making developed, and Wilmington supplied bricks for Henry VIII's manor house in Dartford (1541–4) and before houses were fully constructed of brick it was used for chimneys and fireplaces. At Sutton-at-Hone in 1597, brick was used (with stone for window dressings) for Catherine Wrote's sturdily built almshouses.

The picture generally is of a peaceful domestic countryside. But there was one large military building – Eynsford Castle. It is significant for itself and for its effect on Eynsford, to which it added a second centre. The ford, track-junction and church formed the original nucleus, but the Norman castle requiring an almost 'parade ground' area before its entrance, the main street remains wide at this point today. It is as though Church and State were visibly held in tension, though more probably the Castle was the result of tension within the church for, while Archbishop Lanfranc held Eynsford, his rival Bishop Odo of Bayeux, Earl of Kent, held much of Farningham.

The Castle was probably built soon after Domesday. The son of Ralph, the Domesday holder, was the first of seven Williams of Eynsford, the last of whom held the Castle in 1261. William of Eynsford I became Sheriff of Kent. The building is unusual, if not unique. 'Nowhere in England is there a more complete example of a pre-keep castle' observes John Newman. For this castle had no keep. It consisted basically of a polygonal curtain wall, enclosing an area about 200ft across, within which stood a timber watch-tower, succeeded in the 12th century by a large stone hall-house with solar and undercroft, and an entrance building. The Castle seems to have been dismantled early in the 14th century, and in the 18th century was being used for hunt-kennels by the Hart-Dyke family. Part of the western curtain collapsed during the late 19th century.

The Sybills were also associated with it . When John Sybill died (1574), his widow married Francis Hart of Lullingstone and they lived at Little Mote, the Sybills' Tudor house, close to the Castle. (Later, the Sybills' daughter Elizabeth married Sir Robert Bosvile and, when she died in 1602, the family became extinct).

The foundations of the medieval manor house of Farningham were revealed a few years ago, apparently constructed on a curtain wall and moat dating perhaps from the 13th century, suggesting a castle or a fortified manor house.

The system of Militia Rolls operated through Commissions of Arms, and High Constables notified Lords of Manors. Thus villagers would have been made aware of wars and rumours of wars. They would have heard too of the Cade Rebellion in 1453, for many West Kenters took part, Edmund Chymbham of Southfleet, gentleman, among them. Those later pardoned included Robertus Atte Wode de Asshe juxta Frenyngham, Thomas Pycard of Greenhithe and William Fuller of Stone, yeomen, men with middle-class associations. Jack Cade fled from London to Dartford, and finally to Heathfield, where he was killed by Alexander Iden, Sheriff of Kent. Listed as archers, billmen, and gunners in the West Kent Militia in 1545 were 263 men from twelve Axstane villages. Two-thirds were from Sutton, Southfleet, Eynsford and Horton Kirby. In 1553 Sir Thomas Wyatt raised a force in Kent to protest against Queen Mary's proposed marriage to Philip II of Spain. Robert Rudston of Horton Kirby, Thomas Culpeper, and Thomas Fane (last of the family to hold Scotgrove Manor in Ash) were later confined in the Tower, and their carved inscriptions indicate that they did not expect to survive. 'He that endureth to the end shall be saved' carved Rudston, and 'Be faithful unto death and I will give thee a crown of life. T.Fane, 1553. J. Culpeper'. They were eventually pardoned.

The musters of the Spanish Armada were widespread in their demands for attendance for training, and subsidies were raised from the early 1580s. Under the overall command of Sir John Norris (C-in-C from Kent to Dorset) were Lord Cobham (in command of Kent) with Sir Henry Cobham and Thomas Fane in command of West Kent division, with a reserve of 3,000 men stationed at Maidstone. Three barrels of powder were kept in Dartford, Tonbridge and Sevenoaks; Dartford and Sevenoaks were assembly points for Sutton Lathe. In August the men were disbanded for harvesting, but the alert continued into 1589, while the Musters continued until late in the century, long before which the trained bands were being sent overseas. Billetting, and movement of troops and stores to the port of Gravesend, directly effected the north of Axstane, while recruitment was heavier in Kent in order to save journey time. 'Merrie England' was only half the truth.

This leads to matters of communications. There is a familiar story concerning the mud-filled Sussex track on which an 18th century traveller saw a hat; beneath the hat he found a man, and beneath the man a horse! While North Down tracks were not deep-sunken under heavy Sussex clay, present experience away from metalled lanes shows how difficult even short journeys must have been. Plough-oxen were used to tow the heavy medieval carts and wagons. The main highways – Dover and Maidstone roads – were, except for width, little better than the byways or the routes south towards the Weald, based on the old drove roads. An alternative to the Darent Valley road was that via Romney Street, thence over the Downs' crest to Kemsing. In consequence villages such as Hartley, Ash and Ridley 'enjoyed' an almost complete isolation, especially in winter, and needed to be self-sufficient. With these conditions in mind the Building Accounts of Henry VIII's Manor House at Dartford (1541–4) come to life. Bricks from Wilmington and Horton, timber from Otford, Knole and the Weald, were hauled to the town. Carts of up to two tons' capacity were used, while carters came from Southfleet, Gill's (Darenth), Wilmington, Sutton, Stone and Swanscombe. Local purchases were from Richard Rawlins, churchwarden of Sutton: '13 elmyn trees bought standing at 22d. the piece besides felling, hewing and squaring, carriage ...19 tons at 10d a ton.' and of 'John Carlos of ffarningham for (88) loads of talwood for burning of chawk for lyme.' (Two centuries later, Defoe – who once lived in Hartley – saw 22 oxen hauling an oak on a tug, on the way from Sussex to Chatham Dockyard). Although most of the craftsmen working on the Manor House came from the King's Works no doubt most of the labourers came from within Axstane. At one time 500 men were working on the building.

Communications may not have been considered worthy of first charge on expenditure during the medieval period, but parishes were expected to produce labour annually for road work. Large stone bridges, such as that across the Medway at Rochester, were costly to maintain.

A system of beacons, mainly for defence purposes, is first mentioned in 1324; this was in the Isle of Wight. In 1570 Lambarde in his *Perambulation of Kent* mentions the beacon at Stone, probably the site in Bean of the Old Telegraph Station (Grove Field) shown on the Tithe map (c1840). Tithe map evidence suggests that Rowhill, Wilmington very likely provided the site for another telegraph, though the date for this may be later.

Just as today, however, the main flow of traffic was on the Dover and Maidstone roads. All we have done is to increase the volume and speed (and thereby the tempo of life). But on the hills above Horton, and around Ridley, the sense of medieval remoteness can still be felt.

Deed, confirming exchange of Manor of Darenth for Lambeth, between Prior of Rochester and Archbishop of Canterbury. (KCAO)

ABOVE: Ruins of original Manor House of Fawkham, east of the church. (Cust.Roff) (MJ) LEFT: Medieval glass in Fawkham Church, showing the de Fawkham badge. (Author) RIGHT: Thos de Alkham's 15th century Rectory (much altered). (KCL DD)

ABOVE: The Wrote Almshouses, Sutton-at-Hone (16th century) (later addition to left); left, 19th century Baptist chapel. BELOW: Court Lodge, Horton Kirby c1900; formerly called Horton Castle, but probably a defensive medieval house. (Both ECY/KCL DD)

ABOVE: Court Lodge, Horton Kirby; medieval openings in south wall. (Author) BELOW: Lower Bean Farmhouse. (AC/KCL DD)

ABOVE: Scudder's Farmhouse. (Author) BELOW: Former Royal Oak Inn, Horton Kirby. (KCL DD)

LEFT: Highlands Farm, Swanley. (MJ) RIGHT: Lower Barn End Farmhouse in 1977; originally a yeoman type hall house. (DDAG/KCL DD) BELOW: The Wheatsheaf, Westwood, Southfleet. (RH)

LEFT: The entrance, South Ash Manor. (ECY/KCL DD) RIGHT: Village Stocks, Eynsford, as sited 1904 (since stolen). (HJB/KCL DD) BELOW: South Ash Manor House .

ABOVE: Barn used as Roman Catholic Oratory of St Francis de Sales, Hartley, probably 16th century. (KT) BELOW: Elizabeth, Windmill and Bower Cottages, Eynsford c1900. (ECY/KCL DD)

ABOVE: Franks Hall, Horton Kirby, 16th century: the second building, the first having been sited across the river; 1890. (ECY/KCL DD) BELOW: The Hawley Manor Columbarium, late 16th century: picture taken c1920; building since restored. (KCL DD)

ABOVE: Lullingstone Castle, mid-18th century, showing two gate-houses, moat, and chapel. (KCL DD BL) BELOW: Sutton (formerly Brook) Place. (MJ)

The Church's One Foundation

The churches reflect the centuries more fundamentally in their architecture. The *Textus Roffensis* (c1115), listing churches and chapels which paid rent for chrism oil to the Cathedral, is believed to have been based on pre-Conquest evidence. Of the sixteen original villages only West Kingsdown and Longfield (though no doubt existing) were omitted. Three of the Archbishop's Manors – Darenth, Eynsford and Farningham – were for centuries in Shoreham Deanery, an Archbishop's peculiar.

The original buildings were most likely of timber – rather like Greensted, Essex, with its walls constructed from split trunks. They were probably reconstructed in stone before the Conquest, certainly by the 12th century. Saxon work remains in Darenth, Wilmington, Swanscombe and probably West Kingsdown. The simple two-chamber form of Fawkham, Hartley, Ridley and Lullingstone also suggest Saxon origins, echoed by the known layout of St Margaret Helles, Maplescombe and Lullingst*a*ne. Population increases, religious fervour, Lords of Manors' ambitions, availability of funds, the power of Bishops, all influenced alteration and enlargement of churches. Thus little changed Ridley expresses a quiet backwater parish, while 13th century Horton Kirby and Eynsford suggest collegiate connections, and the 13th century beautifying of Stone church reminds that Bishops of Rochester regularly stayed nearby during their London journeys. The 14th century nave interiors of Ash and Southfleet suggest the influence of Hamo de Hethe (Bishop 1319–52), for Dartford, and Meopham naves were also rebuilt at that time.

Thus this once homogenous group reflected, in their later diversity, religious and social developments while, for students of architecture, they present examples evolving from Saxon to Perpendicular Gothic.

Darenth has remained largely unchanged, probably because it stood by a cross road between two main valley roads where there was little level space for a substantial village to develop. The church stands on a slope, which aids its interior dignity, a dignity increased by the early 12th century stone groined vault over the sanctuary. The north nave wall, its quoins of Roman brick brought from the nearby Roman villa site, and one wide-splay window, are pre-Conquest. A Norman doorway was opened in the wall, but presumably its position was found inconvenient and the present post-medieval porch substituted. In the 12th century a south-east chapel was erected, and in the 13th a south nave aisle and west tower. Later, the chapel was demolished; its arcade remains, incorporated in the south chancel wall. No other Axstane church has, or possibly had, so fine a Romanesque font, carved about 50 years before the Archbishop exchanged the Manor for Lambeth. Were the stone vaulting and font a response to the Archbishop's direct lordship?

Under a Royal Commission of Edward VI, inventories were taken of church goods. In 1553, the Commission for the Lathe, composed of Sir Percyvall Hart, Sir Martin Bowes, Thomas Lovelace and John Browne Esquires, was attended by clergy, churchwardens and principal parishioners. Among Darenth's possessions were two vestments, '3 bells of brass suted [sited] in the steeple' and a 'Bible of the largest volume'; while at the separate chapel of St Margaret Helles was a chalice, 'a Crismatory of tynne remaining in possession of Christopher Draper' and no less than seven vestments.

After the destruction of many chancel screens during the Reformation, altars were not protected from dogs and Archbishop Laud ordered the installation of altar rails. Those at Darenth may be of that 17th century period.

St Margaret Helles chapel was situated near the farmstead. In the later Middle Ages it became difficult to maintain a congregation there, despite Archbishop Warham's directions, most people preferring to worship at the parish church. The chapel gradually fell into decay and there is now no trace of it.

West Kingsdown and Wilmington were originally chapels under Sutton-at-Hone. Wilmington received its first Vicar in 1253 and Kingsdown perhaps rather earlier. About 1445 Kingsdown was converted into a Rectory. Kingsdown was originally a two-chamber building and its nave and tower are possibly late Saxon, the tower's antiquity being emphasised by the heavy use of flint, even for quoins. A narrow arch in its east wall may indicate an apse, as possibly also at Dartford. A low Norman south aisle was added, and later a south chancel chapel. Possibly heavy damage during a great storm in 1223 led to their dismantling. A nave window has on its splays an early 12th century portrayal of the story of Cain and Abel. Two small quatrefoils carry 14th century glass depicting Christ and the Virgin and Child. The 1552 Inventory includes a 'Book of thomelyes [Homilies]' and '1 bell of bras in the steple' (one bell having been sold for the repair of the church). Wilmington's ancient core is in the lower tower, with its two, wide-splayed, probably Saxon windows. The exceptionally plain font may also be of this period. The body of the church has undergone much restoration, Edward Cresy of Horton Kirby tackling the north aisle about 1840, a south aisle being added in 1879, and a new chancel in 1884 (by Ewan Christian). The churchyard tells a continuing story, for many of those buried here played a great part in the public and industrial life of Dartford and Wilmington. A physician to Queen Anne and her two successors, Sir Edward Hulse (died 1759), and Field Marshal Sir Samuel Hulse, lie here, as well as a well-respected Lord of the Manor, Sir James Whitehead (1834-1917), Lord Mayor of London 1888–9.

Even the largely unchanged two-chamber group of churches have gathered elements from succeeding centuries. Fawkham shows its 'deep antiquity' (John Thorpe) in several Norman windows and the probably Norman font bowl, but it has something unique in Axstane, a 13th century wall-painting of the Risen Christ. The following century added a double piscina, and in stained glass, as well as the de Fawkham arms, St Anne teaching the Virgin to read. We should see these things not as from today looking back, but as contemporaries; then may we garner their freshness. Later came the great oak posts supporting the bell-turret (in the 1552 inventory there were two bells; the present single bell was cast in 1604 by Robert Mot of the famous Whitechapel Bell Foundry).

Hartley retains its original door with fine ornamental ironwork; like the nave, it is of the 12th century. The chancel was rebuilt in the 13th century and in the south wall there are a mass-dial and low-side window (the latter probably where the Sanctus bell was rung, to remind those outside of the moment of elevation of the Host). The building then remained unchanged for about 600 years. Only in the late 19th century was restoration effected — a new east wall and vestry, a west wall and bell–turret (based on a drawing of 1806). The font seems a mixture of 13th and 15th century work; Jacobean, the pulpit (the simplest of designs again reminding us of a humble village). The 1552 inventory said simply: '1 chalice . . . stolen'. By the 18th century the rectory may have become as neglected as the church; in 1786 Rector Thomas Bradley sought permission to reside outside the parish (in Greenhithe) as the rectory was so dilapidated. It was eventually rebuilt on Hoseland Hill near the Longfield boundary.

Ridley retains its Norman nave (lengthened probably when the porch was built and the weather-boarded turret erected c1830). A chancel chapel was added in the 13th century, but the chancel was restored in the 19th. Any optimism towards an increase in population was unjustified; while numbers rose from 47 (1801) to 101 (1861), there was then a decline to 73 (1921).

Lullingstone is a unique experience in Axstane. Virtually the family chapel of the Peche, Hart and Hart Dyke families, it has remarkable stained glass, that of the 15th century showing the Peche arms (motto: 'Prest a faire' (alert, or quick to do)). Sir John Peche's refurbishing early in Henry VIII's reign, with the fine screen bearing the Aragon pomegranate and the symbolic peach, and the north chapel, prepared the interior for transformation from medieval to Renaissance character, which the plaster ceiling and chequered floor of Percyvall Hart (died 1738) richly completed. The tiny, encased marble font, possibly late 17th century, is exceedingly rare. The memorials are so much part of the church and they illustrate the changing styles of tombs down the centuries. Sir John Peche's tomb stands between the sanctuary and north chapel; its design is midway between the medieval and Renaissance periods. South of the sanctuary the Renaissance tomb of Sir Percyvall Hart, nephew of Sir John Peche, dominates. In the chapel Sir George Hart's monument (1603) dispenses with the upper storey, but the tomb-chest has four small standing figures representing labour, peace, death and resurrection. Opposite stands an 18th century Gothic-Rococo monument to the church's 'munificent repairer and beautifier' Percyvall Hart though, in view of his work on the chapel, one wonders whether the memorial would have been his choice. Anne Dyke (née Hart) who died in 1763, has a marble wall monument both dignified and charming.

Humbly, outside in the church's north shadow, is the simple grave-stone to the Rt Hon Sir William Hart Dyke Bart PC (died 1931, aged 94). Born in Queen Victoria's accession year, an MP 1868-1906 (for Dartford constituency from 1885), he served under Disraeli and became Secretary for Ireland, although probably his greatest work was in education. His last public engagement, in March 1931, was the opening of the Dartford West Central (now Secondary) Schools.

Lullingstone's 1552 inventory shows '1 bell in the steple excepte 1 bell whereof a cloke is nowe made for the commoditie of the parishe'.

Maplescombe is now only a pile of rubble shrouded in bushes by the track to High Castle Wood. It was a single-chamber, apsidal Norman building, mainly of flint with some Roman brick. As late as 1917 a 13th century window could be seen in the west gable. The church was already falling into decay when the 1552 inventory reported the 'little bell of bras broken with the fallyng downe oute of the saide steple decayed about ij yeres last past' and though it still had a silver chalice 'grav'd with the picture of our Lord' all other goods had been stolen. The last Rector was instituted in 1610 and a little later the parish was united with Kingsdown.

Eynsford, Horton Kirby and Stone are all of the 13th century Early English style, yet they vary markedly. Norman detail remains in all three; at St Martin of Tours, Eynsford, the west doorway, masonry in the nave south wall and traces of windows in the chancel; at St Mary, Horton Kirby, a few carved remnants set in the west wall, and at St Mary, Stone, the re-positioned entrance doorway.

Eynsford is remarkable for its tall lancet windows in both wide chancel and south transept, but especially for its apse, possibly based on the Norman plan. The north chapel is Tudor. 'Fear God, honour the King' says the George III coat-of-arms motto.

Horton Kirby is a diminution of its former self. The building is probably late 12th century (round arches headed the aisles, and stone – not marble – was used for the lancets' slender shafting). There were arcaded aisles as well as transepts, a chancel double the present length, and a broach spire. When in 1379 the Rectory was acquired by the Cobhams and a Vicar was installed, the incumbent's income was severely reduced. Probably to economise on maintenance, the aisles were dismantled. But the greater tragedy was the destruction of the east half of the chancel in

1816–17, when the broach spire and tower were also taken down, the tower rebuilt in brick. Even so, the high aspiring crossing- arches, the still dignified chancel, and the transepts' arcading, add grace to St Mary's.

Stone is certainly unique in Axstane – and for many miles further. The church was so admired by G.E.Street, architect of the London Law Courts that, when he restored it, he charged no fee. The Early English work starts east of the tower, with tall slender columns incorporating Purbeck marble shafts. Detail grows progressively elaborate eastwards. Street dismantled the Perpendicular style chancel windows and replaced them with windows of the original 13th century design. Below them is the original Early English foliage work c1260, probably carved in Westminster Abbey masons' yard. The connection of the Bishops of Rochester with Stone suggests their influence. Above, the chancel was originally stone-vaulted (taken down c1640).

The tower was a later addition, and the nave aisles were lengthened to embrace it, while to support it, massive 14th century multi-shafted Decorated style piers, with foliage capitals, were constructed. In 1473 John Bokelond left money for paving the way from the chancel to the west door, and for 'new schynglyng' the roof. In 1526 Sir John Wiltshire's chapel, containing his tomb, was added north of the chancel. The 1552 inventory mentions 'iij bells in the steple suted of brasse, on saint's bell. . . and two sacryeng bells. . .' and 'on vestment of red damaske. . . the gift of Sir John Wilshire Knyghte'.

At Farningham the church is mainly Early English, though on a humbler scale than Eynsford, to whose Rectory it was but a Vicarage. Three lancet windows in the chancel indicate the arrangement, and the chancel arch is flanked by small blank arches containing lancets. Its own unique possession in Axstane is the seven sacrament font, of a 15th century, mainly East Anglian, tradition. The tower's traditionally Kentish appearance, with staircase turret, is misleading; a drawing of 1796 shows it lacking a top-stage. Although the 1552 inventory shows '3 bells suted in the stepple' it may have been taken down. One was added in 1830. The inventory also included a 'Paraphrase of Erasmus, 70 lbs of old brasse to be sold for repair of the church'. Some of the 19th century stained glass was designed by Charles Winston, son of a former Vicar. His important contribution to the revival of this art is acknowledeged in the *Encyclopaedia Britannica*.

Swanscombe is a hybrid, but a worthy one. Despite 19th century restoration and a disastrous fire (1902) its development charts an enduring history. Probably commencing as a Saxon two-cell building, a pre-Conquest tower was added, the lower part – including a window incorporating Roman tiles – remaining. The Normans largely rebuilt the church. Here also are blank arches flanking the chancel arch. In the late 12th century they added aisles and a nave clerestory, and lengthened the chancel. The tower was largely reconstructed in the 13th century, while the chancel arch is 14th century. Continuous development then, as the community grew. Yet the early font, now sadly worn, but once finely carved, still survives. One hesitates to use the word 'unique' once more, but the medieval (15th century) lectern demands it. The early brass candelabra is dated 1687, and the pulpit is 18th century. Each century has made a contribution which restoration and fire have not despoiled. The 1872–3 restoration was heavy, and later a new porch was given by Sir Erasmus Wilson, FRS (died 1884), whose tomb stands in the north aisle. Sir Erasmus, a famous surgeon, is popularly remembered because he was instrumental in bringing the Egyptian obelisk, Cleopatra's Needle, to England.

Nothing remains of the original Saxon or Norman churches of Ash or Southfleet. Both are large and in outward form not dissimilar. Ash, however, retains its basically 13th century tower and Early English chancel, though this chancel has a simple plainness. The nave was rebuilt during the 14th century with a north aisle terminating in the Lady Chapel partly alongside the chancel. The crown-post roof is contemporary. The south aisle was probably widened in 1472, when a bequest was made for nave work; here was the chapel of St Blaise. Ash's inventory of 1552 included two chalices and nothing more, some items having been stolen. Many ledger slabs of the 16th to 18th centuries, relating to the Hodsolls of South Ash, form the floor of the centre aisle and Lady Chapel. (Close by the church is the 17th century Manor House.)

The dedication of St Nicholas, Southfleet reinforces the tradition of the River Ebbsfleet, linking the village with the Thames and sea. This church is completely of the Decorated (early 14th century) period. The narrow tower, its upper stages markedly set back from those below, attracts attention. The 14th century door leads the feet on to the deliberately positioned grave-slab immediately within. The spacious interior – chancel especially so – may reflect the importance which the Diocese attached to this living. The stone altar slab, with its five consecration crosses, survived the Reformation by being buried in the churchyard. The 15th century font's eight sides are symbolically carved, and the bishop portrayed may be St Nicholas of Myra. Among the choirstalls are misericords, and some early pews remain. The pulpit is early Jacobean while the fine 12-branch candelabra of 1768 adds a delicate dignity. The 1552 inventory lists 27 items, including two chalices, a great and two little candlesticks of latten, 'iiij bells of bronze suted and ij handbells of brasse', eight vestments and five copes, one of which was 'imbrothered [embroidered] with lambes of Venys [Venice] gold'. A deacon and sub-deacon are mentioned, so there were apparently three clergy. The south aisle became known as the Scadbury pew and the north aisle the Hook Place pew, for the Swan family.

St John the Baptist, Sutton, like St Peter and St Paul, Ash, was rebuilt in the early 14th century, with a later, typically Kentish, tower with stair-turret. The window tracery is of a particularly flowing design. Alas, in 1615 this church, like Swanscombe, suffered fire. The new furnishings were inevitably Jacobean, including the pulpit (almost identical to Dartford's), reading desk and tower screen. Heavy 19th century restoration had a mixed effect; substitution of the 14th century arcade by marble columns and coarse foliage was unfortunate, but the window tracery was restored in its original form.

Last of the early foundations is Longfield. This still retains a Norman window, incorporated in a 13th century chancel, while a north aisle and arcade formed a late medieval enlargement. But with the population trebling from 113 to 328 between 1821 and 1881, further enlargement was authorised and the nave was lengthened and a tower added. John Currey, Dartford's longest serving Vicar (1778–1825) was Rector of Longfield, as his wall monument in Dartford Church testifies.

These then are the ancient churches of Axstane. They, of all the buildings in the Hundred, enshrine most clearly the story of the villages. These lines provide but a hint of what may be garnered from their store of local information As exemplars of styles of architecture, monuments and furnishings, they have a wider bearing, emphasising yet again that Axstane did not develop within a vacuum. 'No man is an island, entire of itself' wrote John Donne; neither is a village, nor yet a Hundred.

Darenth Church, (St Margaret) from south-east. (ECY/KCL DD)

ABOVE LEFT: Darenth Church interior c1840 (from a watercolour). (MJ) RIGHT: The Chapel of St Margaret Helles, Darenth in the 18th century. (Cust.Roff). ECY/KCL DD) BELOW LEFT: West Kingsdown Church (St Edmund King and Martyr), from south. (MJ) RIGHT: Farningham Church (SS Peter and Paul); the 15th century seven sacraments font. (KCL DD)

LEFT: Swanscombe Church (SS Peter and Paul) from west, (CT) and ABOVE: after fire, 14 August 1902. BELOW: Fawkham Church from south-west c1900. (Both ECY/KCL DD)

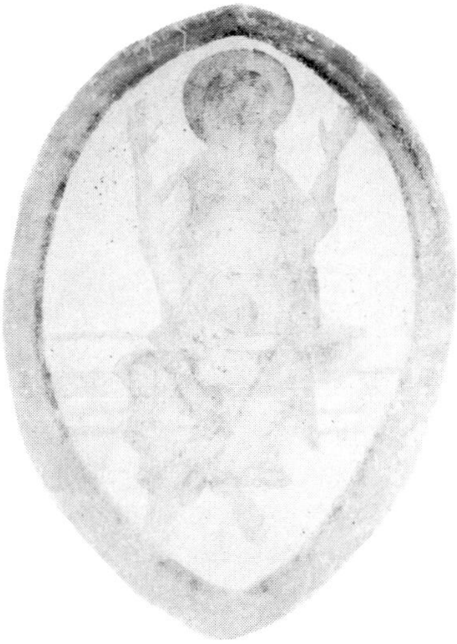

LEFT: Fawkham Church, 13th century painting of the Risen Christ. (MJ) RIGHT: Hartley Church (All Saints) from south-east. (DGR) INSET: Hartley Church, mass-dial. (MJ) BELOW: Ridley Church and Court Lodge Farmhouse (Author).

ABOVE: Longfield Church (St Mary Magdalene) 1888. (CY/KCL DD)
BELOW: Ruins of Lullingstane Chapel in 18th century. (Cust.Roff.) (KCL DD)

ABOVE LEFT: Lullingstone Church (St Botolph), from south-west, c1960. (KCL DD) RIGHT: Horton Kirby Church (St Mary), c1800. (Note spire and double-length chancel and porch). (MG) CENTRE LEFT: Horton Kirby church pre-1957, when battlements were dismantled. (MG) RIGHT: Southfleet Church, (St Nicholas), interior. (MJ) BELOW: Ash Church (SS Peter and Paul), and 17th century Manor House. (ECY/DGR)

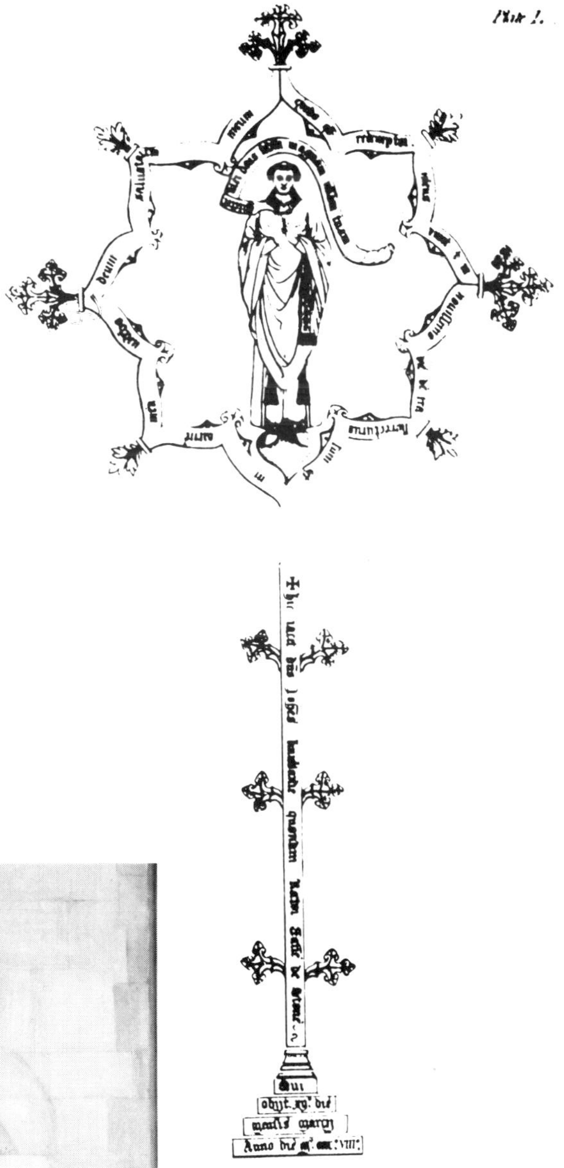

ABOVE LEFT: Stone Church (St Mary) interior, early 19th century (drawn and engraved by W.S.Wilkinson): note Perpendicular style east window; (KCL DD) RIGHT: Brass to Rev John Lambard(e), Rector 1408–18; (Cust.Roff.) (MJ) BELOW LEFT: Late 13th century wall-painting of murder of Archbishop Becket, 1170 — watercolour by Professor Tristram, showing its state when he inspected it earlier this century and RIGHT: 13th century Early English dragon decoration in chancel arcading. (Both MJ)

LEFT: Southfleet Church; tomb of John Sedley, 1605 and CENTRE: tomb of Sir Raphe Weldon, 1609. RIGHT: Sutton-at-Hone Church; tomb of Sir Thomas Smythe, 1625. BELOW: Southfleet Free School founded 1637, here in the 18th century. (Cust. Roff). (All MJ)

Family Matters

Just as the Reformation transformed the religious scene, so Henry VIII's break with the Papacy revived the spirit of national independence. Internally, Parliament and the County Justices were growing in importance while feudal ties were weakening. Parliament needed a single authority for each locality. In the absence of any other central civil authority within the parish the Incumbent and Churchwardens, meeting together with parishioners in Vestry, were the automatic choice for this function. Among the secular duties of Sutton-at-Hone churchwardens were: freeing the parish of vermin, acting as relieving officers, assisting disabled soldiers to return home, providing alms for the poor, organising collections of money for assisting parishes affected by disaster (the former Papal Briefs), and paying for bell-ringing on national occasions.

A new loyalty was thus erected and the next three centuries brought more and more secular burdens on to the shoulders of essentially religious bodies, while the suppression of the monasteries meant closure of institutions which hitherto helped the poor. Nevertheless the manor remained of social importance, and many still alive can recall their elders speaking with respect, even deference, of 'the gentry'. Much still depended on the benevolence and will of the Lord of the Manor. He might well be a national figure, like Sir Thomas Smythe at Sutton-at-Hone, or hold office at Court like Sir Raphe and Sir Anthony Weldon (Swanscombe), or be a friend of Royalty as Percyvall Hart of Lullingstone. He still had tradition and wealth on his side, and if he held the advowson of the clerical living his standing was enhanced. So inheritance of the lordship continued to be of great significance, especially in small communities. In 1640 nearly half the gentry in north-west Kent had settled there since 1603.

About 1619 Sir Thomas Smythe acquired a moiety of Sutton Manor (formerly held by the Wrotes) together with Brook (later Sutton) Place. He also acquired the Manor of Grandisons alias Wilmington, formerly held by Sir Thomas Moyle, and bought Rowhill. He died at Brook Place in 1625 and his Renaissance tomb stands proudly in Sutton church. Sir Thomas had been Commissioner of the Navy, Sheriff of London, First Governor of the East India Company, and Ambassador to Russia. His intrepid travels led him to the Amazon, and he encouraged exploration of the North-West Passage, where his name remains in Smith's Sound; over 200 years later Sir John Franklin sailed from Greenhithe on the same search. Sir Thomas left many charitable bequests – to London hospitals, Tonbridge School (founded by his grandfather), while Smythe's Charity benefits 14 parishes including Sutton-at-Hone. The family held Sutton Place until about 1699, but in 1778 and 1790 the last of the line, Sir Sidney Stafford Smythe and his widow, were brought here for burial.

The 1699 purchaser was Sir John Lethieullier, a wealthy City merchant, of a family who came from Brabant, probably during the 16th century. Two years earlier Sir John had bought Wilmington and Rowhill, which the family held with the Sutton property until 1766. Thus for about 150 years two families in succession exerted great influence on the social life of two neighbouring villages.

John Mumford purchased the same properties in 1767, and, with the purchase of St John's (including St John's Ash) in 1780, re-united the Sutton Manors for the first time for 200 years. His descendants, by marriage with the Campbells (of West Kingsdown) and Fleet families continued this dominating influence into the 20th century. Some can recall Algernon Fleet riding his tall chestnut bay into Dartford from Darenth Grange during the 1920s.

Near Sir Thomas Smythe's tomb is a tablet to Abraham Hill (1635–1721), who in 1667 acquired St John's Jerusalem. He was a Commissioner for Trade, Comptroller to the Archbishop of Canterbury (the famous Dr Tillotson), and a founder member and Treasurer of the Royal Society, (and thus an acquaintance of Boyle and Newton). He added two almshouses to the Wrote foundation, and tried to introduce cider-apple growing to Sutton. A later relative was an absentee landlord who let St John's to Edward Hasted, famous historian of Kent, who made considerable alterations to the house, virtually converting it to its present appearance. Fortunately he retained the chancel of the Commandery church which the building originally was. Hasted married Ann Dorman of Sutton, who died in 1803 and was buried there. He died at Corsham, Wilts, in 1812.

As Wilmington and Sutton show, linkage between manors of various parishes continued. About 1603, Elizabeth, daughter of George Killingworth, married Christopher Eglesfield, to whom she brought Hackstaple (Hextable). By 1691, when Nicholas Searle died, the family had acquired the Lord's Goss (for £115) and held 240 acres in Sutton and Wilmington parishes. Hextable was conveyed to Charles Egerton c1733. Egerton was a descendant of Thomas Egerton, Master of the Mint 1553–4. A tenant in 1795 was Dr David Pitcairn, a member of the Royal Society. The Egertons held Hextable until 1876 (by which time Swanley was a separate parish), and the house was demolished after 1945. Gilden Hill passed from the Harts of Lullingstone to the Boteler family of Teston in James I's time; they also held one of the Fawkham manors until 1772, when they were bequeathed to Elizabeth, Viscountess Folkestone, and came to the Bouverie family, one of whom took the name of Pusey.

Highlands in Swanley and Franks, Horton Kirby, remained with the Bathursts until Francis died in 1738; his grand-daughter Joyce married John Tasker of Dartford. In 1766 Highlands was sold to John Calcraft of Ingress, Greenhithe, an ambitious man who hoped for a peerage but was denied one by an early death. Highlands was bought in 1787 by John Mumford of Sutton. In 1796 John Tasker died, but his second wife Anne Faunce was still living at Franks in 1797.

Edward Bathurst demolished what was probably the first Wilmington Manor House (at Barn End); he built another on Wilmington Common, later Wilmington Hall.

Hawley, after passing through various hands, was granted by William III in 1695 to Sir Francis Leigh, who had purchased Cleyndon (Darenth) in 1691. Richard, son of Richard Leigh, Serjeant-at-Law, married Elizabeth Mumford. The Leigh's descendants held Hawley Manor until modern times. Thomas Rolt's widow sold Helles in Darenth to George Gifford of Eynsford and Fawkham in the late 17th century. In 1713 it was divided (with his other estates) between Gifford's three daughters, one marrying Francis Leigh of Hawley (1722), but all three moieties were conveyed to John Lane (leatherseller), whose family name is no doubt preserved in Lane's (or Lane) End, Darenth. Sir Richard Lane held St Margaret's in 1781, but in 1788 it was alienated to Christopher Chapman, who held the main Manor.

Horton Castle (Court Lodge) went by marriage from Rudstone to Michel of Old Windsor in James I's reign but, in 1736, there being no heirs, John Michel left the estate to the Queen's College, Oxford. The Manor of Kirby Court (later the Hall) went from Sir Thomas Walsingham to Alderman Cuthbert Hackett (Lord Mayor 1626), then through various hands, including the Polhill family. In 1749 it was conveyed to Richard Hornsby, a Sheriff of Kent, but in 1792 was sold to Edward Homewood. Reynolds Place, Horton Kirby, (its house much reduced in size after the great storm of 1703) was held in the 15th century by the Brownes (two Lord Mayors among them).

In Charles I's reign it was sold to Sir John Jacob, then to Sir Harbottle Grimston Bart (Speaker, and later Master of the Rolls); he sold it to Sir John Beale (c1684), who held Farningham. His daughter married Sir George Heyer and this family held Reynolds Place until 1774, the year after Gabriel Heyer (Lord Coleraine) died.

During the Middle Ages the de Frenyngham and the Isleys held the four Farningham Manors, except for a portion of Charton. In the 16th century the Sybills held Chimbhams, but in 1763 Joseph Cox bought it. The main Farningham manor, together with Petham Place and part of Charton, went to the Ropers, relatives of Sir Thomas More. The rest of Charton went to the Martyns and Bathursts of Franks. The Ropers were succeeded by Sir John Cotton. A later owner conveyed Petham Place to Sir Edward Bathurst, and it later descended to Calcraft of Ingres and to Sir John Dyke. Farningham was conveyed to Sir John Beale, to whom came Cotton's portion of Charton.

Eynsford became closely linked with the Lullingstone families, and Orkesden was sold in the 18th century to Sir Percival Hart. Little Mote continued with the Bosviles until the mid-18th century. In 1755 the house was purchased by Benjamin Harvey, a maltster. Petham Court was held consecutively by the Sybills and Bosviles, becoming linked with Pole (Southfleet) and Gilden Hill (Swanley). Pole went by marriage to Sir Robert Marsham Bart, whose son became the first Lord Romney. This family held Petham Court until 1806.

Most of Kingsdown descended from Richard Lovelace (died 1658) to Henry Coke. Last of this family to hold Kingsdown was the famed agriculturalist, Coke of Norfolk, and in 1784 the property was sold to Duncan Campbell, prosperous City merchant of the Mount, Wilmington, who married Mary Mumford of Sutton Place.

South Ash Manor House, long held by the Hodsolls, stands in isolated half-timbered splendour. Ralph de Hodeshole held land in the district as early as 1198. The Hodsolls succeeded the Southesshe family. The fifth William Hodsoll (died 1776) was a notable cricketer. After 1799 the family unexpectedly declined.

The Manor of North Ash (now the New Ash Green area) reverted to the Crown on Sir Edward Moynings' death (1523); first Thomas Cromwell, then Sir Martin Bowes followed. The Manor House (Ash Place) is close by the church; it came to Sir Edmund Fowler and (1718) to Multon Lambarde, of the *Perambulation of Kent* author's family. He also held Ridley, Haliwell and defunct Scotgrove, and the advowson, and his descendant continues here today. New Fawkham (Pennis) mansion was rebuilt by Thomas Walter in Elizabeth I's reign; it was sold to George Gifford in the 1660s and later it went by marriage to John Selby (the Ightham family).

Longfield's Rochester connections included Archdeacon Thomas Plume (died 1704), founder of a Chair of Astronomy at Cambridge and a great benefactor. Pepys writes of him as 'a very excellent scholar and preacher'. He is buried at Longfield.

The Sedleys continued at Scadbury, Southfleet. John Sedley's large Renaissance monument stands in the church. In 1637 Sir John Sedley left £500 for founding a Free School, part of which is still standing. In the 18th century, however, the family exchanged Southfleet for lands elsewhere.

At Hook Place in 1608 was Sir William Swan, who married Meriell Champneis, daughter of Justinian Champneis of Hall Place, Bexley. In 1667 another Sir William, gentleman of the Privy Chamber and Resident at Hamburg, maintained the wharf at Greenhithe for the Navy. The family sold Hook Place to the Harringtons in 1701, whence it descended to the Russells and Brooks.

At Swanscombe Sir Raphe Weldon (died 1609), Chief Clerk of the Kitchens to Elizabeth I and Clerk Controller to James I, and his son Anthony – also in Royal service – have their Renaissance tombs; Sir Raphe's is particularly ornate. On Walker Weldon's death (1731) his heirs sold to Thomas Blechynden. By 1800 Swanscombe was held by Lord Ducie. Combs (Alkerden) was variously held until being sold to David Powell c1795. Ingress came in 1748 to Viscount Duncannon (Earl of Besborough 1758); after 1761 to John Calcraft, and later to the Roebuck family.

During the 17th and 18th centuries Littlebrook (Stone) was held by the Appletons and Potters. Stone Castle's 17th century holders included the Carews and Archdeacon Dr Plume. The lessee in 1797 was John Talbot, related to the Taskers. Cotton was held by a Keeper of the Seal, and later by a Master of the Temple. Stone Place went through various hands, and in 1797 was held by William Tuckey of Greenhithe.

Even this incomplete picture of manorial holdings shows a society disciplined by land-ownership, an ownership important in relations with Government and in the balancing of authority between King and Parliament. Not the Civil War (1642–6), the Glorious Revolution (1688), nor the problems attending the American War of Independence, resolved this question. Meanwhile the parson was often the link between rich and poor.

Swanley remained an example of an area of mostly small farms with no manorial lord. The first Swanley entry in the Sutton registers was in 1618, but the hamlet was long recognised as an almost separate entity, and one of the two churchwardens was from the 'Swanley side', and several Borsholders were appointed for the two 'sides'. In 1747 separate churchwardens' accounts were produced. A Court was held for Sutton Place in 1733 for which many Swanley tenants were listed.

Coldharbour (alias Soranks) Farm, in the parishes of Sutton, Horton Kirby, and Farningham, had been acquired by Lord Romney; the Daltons belonged to a yeoman family of that name and, when Samuel Dalton died (1697), that estate was split into Upper and Lower Daltons – 'The Old Place' of 1876 was built on Lower Dalton land. Thomas Williams, Dartford solicitor, eventually bought out the Dalton family.

The Old College took its name from Cobham College. The earliest known holder of the Orchard Estate (near the Old College) was John Hornsby, Steward to Sir Joseph Williamson (died 1701) of Cobham Hall. Sir Joseph left Hornsby a third of his estates. Hornsby built Kirby Court (the Hall) in 1738 and let the Orchard Estate; in 1792 John Staples bought it. Staples, a yeoman, was tenant of New Barn Farm in Swanley. A later John Staples occupied Highlands Farm (1824–48) and was easily Swanley's most important man. Tiny Lucas Farm took its name from 18th century Richard Lucas, a Lethieullier overseer.

Nemefield (top of Highlands Hill), was originally a 15th–16th century yeoman's house linked to Highlands Farm. Part of Nemefield later became a forge, which Matthew Saxton occupied in 1666. Opposite, on Potcher's Bank, stood another yeoman's house.

Five Wents (*Wents* meaning ways is found elsewhere in Axstane) became part of the Romney Estate. Three cottages stood on Goss Hill (the Lord's Goss) in 1780. The Poorhouse, probably late 17th century, stood at the top of Highlands Hill. The Land Tax Assessment of 1780 shows the fragmentary nature of this hamlet's lands.

Mid-17th century Wilmington had only four large houses: Bodman's Place (now Wilmington House) occupied by the Twisletons, a Dartford family who succeeded John Beer; Shirehall (the Harmans); and the Barn End residences of Lancelot Bathurst and Francis Langworth. The Hearth Tax Return shows 58 houses, and a population of about 240. Birchwood Road was Ffayrepitte Lane, Shirehall Lane was Oakesland Lane, and Oakfield Lane was Tinkerpot Lane (another Tinkerpot Lane is still in Kingsdown). Below Barn End was Wheaturshe Lane, part of Church Way from Stanhill to Wilmington Church, crossed by Styleways (now Stock) Lane.

In 1637 Anne Braythwayte of Wilmington married Lancelot Bathurst of Franks and Barn End, at Sutton Church and, on her death (1668), she bequeathed the Bathurst charity. Edward

Bathurst, who demolished the Barn End mansion and built Common House (later Wilmington Hall, inherited Finchcocks (Goudhurst) in 1718 and rebuilt that house. The Austens, distant relatives of Jane, succeeded the Bathursts at the Hall. The last Langworth buried in Wilmington died in 1721. The Harmans were a yeoman family for 300 years, and several were churchwardens. There were cherry orchards and flocks of sheep in Wilmington then. John White's blacksmith's shop was well tooled-up; his cottage included a buttery and brewery: total value £39 15s 8d. Stephen Perry, who died 1736, bought Shirehall and built the Mount (Mount Pleasant). He was involved in an unseemly contest over his right to a church pew; he lost the court case and the Vicar wrote of him: 'that great enemy to the church and clergy'. Later, Duncan Campbell leased the Mount from Thurston Ford, and (1784) bought the Coke estates in Kingsdown. John Twisleton died in 1757; after a law-suit his Wilmington House estate went to John Tasker, Dartford brewer, who restored the house.

The church registers record soldiers of the Dartford Heath camp during the American Revolutionary War. A workhouse was established in 1777.

During this 200 years there were only nine Vicars, three of them buried at Wilmington. The most noteworthy was Samuel Denne (1767–99) also Vicar of Darenth. He was an antiquary and correspondent of Hasted, Thorpe, and Dr Latham, discoverer of the Dartford Warbler.

The villages were closely related through individuals. The name Scudder was well-known in the district during the 16th to 18th centuries. As early as 1451 Thomas Scudder lived in Horton Kirby, in 'Olde Scudders', possibly the present house in Fawkham Valley road. Among properties left by William Scudder (will, 1607) was a malt-house in Frog Lane, Sutton; and he left bequests to the poor of Darenth, Sutton and Horton Kirby. In 1635 Thomas Scudder settled in Massachusetts and there is now a Scudder Association in America.

In 1643 the religious quarrel touched Darenth, for Rev Robert Warburton was apparently ejected and Rev J.Larkin substituted. Under the 1662 Act, Rev John Davis was ejected. No Vicars of Bray these. A Parliamentary Commission of 1650 found Larkin's successor, Martin Cacket, 'preached and taught every Lord's Day, but to little edification. . .'. Edmund Davenport of Green Street Green was a familiar figure in Darenth during the mid–17th century; he gave the Royal Arms of Charles II and other gifts to the church. He lived at Clock House, where there was an ice-house, sometimes referred to as 'The Dungeons'. (There were other ice-houses at Darenth Grange and near Wilmington Hall.)

Trendle Down or Trenley Down (once Tyrlingdown) was formerly (c1365) a Cobham estate. 'The Gore' was the home of William Lee, Surveyor to the Navy in Queen Anne's reign; his wife's memorial is dated 1746.

Links between Darenth and Horton Kirby were evidenced when in 1774 the churchwardens and overseers of the poor in both parishes considered an agreement to found a joint workhouse, presumably that on the west side of Lane's End of the long Green Street Green. Darenth workhouse being sold in 1792, Horton Kirby made a new arrangement with Southfleet in 1793. Darenth then possibly used Sutton or Dartford Workhouses. In any case twenty village workhouses were incoporated in 1836 in the Dartford Union Workhouse. Three packs of hounds hunted the neighbourhood; in 1781 Sir Richard Lane had 'full power to hunt, hawk, fish, and fowl, etc.'.

In 1615 occurred the dramatic fire which wrecked Sutton Church; it was caused by someone using a gun to drive a bird from the tower. In 1628 Thomas Terry of Shoreham left a cottage at Dean Bottom (Horton) for the benefit of the poor of Sutton and Horton Kirby. Vicar Hazelwood (1622–55) apparently successfully rode the religious tight-rope between Charles I and Cromwell. Many succeeding Vicars held other livings as well; Hazelwood's successor Hopkins was also Rector of Swanscombe. In 1665 came Dr Stradling, mentioned by Pepys and Evelyn. Peter Mews (Vicar 1670–85) was also Dean of Rochester and (1672) Bishop of Bath and Wells, possibly rewards for his being wounded fighting for Charles I. During his (probably absentee) vicariate the Vicarage was rebuilt (there were both Vicarage and Parsonage in Sutton).

The Rookery Estate at Hawley was held (1652) by Sarah, Countess Dowager of Leicester, but went (1667) to Thomas Gifford MD, of Fawkham, and in 1711 Francis Leigh was involved; Francis was the son of Sir Francis Leigh, who held Hawley Manor.

Hawley paper mill, probably originally a flour mill, was established before 1758, when Christopher Jarrett & Co held it. In 1762 William Archer held it and about 1785 John Hall of Dartford, engineer, was employed.

Edmund Barrell, Vicar of Sutton in 1705, was son of a Recorder of Rochester, and was Rector of Fawkham 1712–20. Interested in science, he recorded twice sighting the Aurora Borealis from the Vicarage, and an earthquake felt at Lullingstone. He was well acquainted with Abraham Hill and Hasted. His grandson Edward Faunce was Vicar for 25 years, holding Horton Kirby also 1763–70; his successor Robert Fountaine (1787–1818) also held both livings. 113 years for 3 vicars!

In 1745 a Brief raised in respect of a fire at Eynsford raised 8s 11½d from Sutton. At the 1767 sale of Sutton Place a corn mill and a hop garden were recorded.

John Swarland, Horton Kirby's first married Vicar, died in 1627. He and his predecessor covered 66 years. Anthony Roper of Farningham, grandson of Sir Thomas More, left a bequest for the poor of Farningham and Horton Kirby. During the Civil War and Commmonwealth and even beyond, Vicars failed to keep proper records; Horton baptism register 1639–61 shows only one name; no marriages were recorded 1643–82, and only one burial 1648–70. In 1688 Anne Collyers was to be cured by the King's touch of scrofula, but this precious right was not proceeded with. 'the chirurgeon's affirming it was not the King's Evil'. Vicar Henry Barrow refused to acknowledge William III and Mary II, and was ejected as a non-Juror.

During the early 18th century Francis Bathurst tragically lost three wives; Susanne (1707), Martha (1721), and Frances (1725). Another tragedy occurred a few years later, when Thomas Polhill and his family, of Kirby Court, were poisoned by Dr Gill Smith, who also murdered his own wife. Smith, a surgeon at Dartford Workhouse (1732) was hanged on Kennington Common in 1738. In 1770 Thomas Williams bought the patronage of the living and appointed his brother Richard as Vicar (1770–1801).

The Foots Cray–Wrotham Heath section of the Maidstone road was turnpiked in 1752, and in 1766 the Dartford–Sevenoaks road. The Dartford–Northfleet section of the Dover Road was turnpiked in 1760. The Ightham turnpike branched south from the Maidstone road near Terry's Lodge, beyond which was a tollgate. The Maidstone and Sevenoaks roads crossed at Farningham, where the bridge was rebuilt in 1773 and widened in 1833. There was a tollgate on Beast (now Gorse) Hill. From Dartford, the first tollgate was at the junction with Church Hill, Wilmington, and another south of the early 19th century poor house at Farningham, which was apparently superseded by the Frog Lane (Devon Road) gate at Sutton-at-Hone. There was also a bar at Darenth. The road turned south from Farningham at White Post, and approached the Eynsford Gate. The road to Lullingstone and Shoreham Castle west of the river had a bar covering the Crockenhill road; this lane, avoiding the main turnpike, was termed Sparepenny Lane. The Lullingstone stretch was closed by Sir Pervical Hart Dyke in 1861 and diverted from Kingfisher Bridge to the main road.

As well as stage-coaches, there were carrier's waggons and carts, and the heavy waggons carrying timber, chalk, agricultural produce – and paper from the Eynsford mill. There were also balloon waggons with their hooped canvas covers. Horses were changed at the Lion Hotel and the (Pied) Bull Inn (the latter catering for the public coaches). The Hop Pole at Button Street (1828) became a regular stopping place for Swanley travellers.

Farningham's linear layout is dictated by the London road, and the village extended along it.

Much rebuilding took place during the 18th century, encouraged by the coaching traffic. Small wonder that, with its horse-fair and market, Farningham considered town status, although Eynsford had twice its population. The Lion existed in 1721, as probably did the massive supposed boundary arches, which bestride the river. The fine weatherboarded mill and elegant mill-house were held until 1774 by the Lord of the Manor, but in 1797 were occupied by Henry Colyer, of a family who held a mill in Dartford. Mount Pleasant, in Sparepenny Lane, was built about 1720. The Bricklayers' Arms (opposite the end of the Lane) was built about 1805.

In 1616 Beesfield (part of Charton Manor) was referred to as Bestfield (John Best then held it). The Parsonage was leased by the Dean and Chapter of Rochester from 1417 to 1737. Sir John Fullerton and Bourchier Cleeve of Foots Cray Place were connected with the property. Thomas Nash, who died in 1778, may have had his churchyard mausoleum designed by his nephew, John Nash, the famous architect. In 1792 the Poor Rate was 1s 6d in the £, but collections were made in addition. Until 1805 Farningham had no poor-house and the parish used the Sutton Poor-house.

In 1629 Rector of Eynsford John Gifford was chaplain to Charles I. In 1629 Thomas Terry's charity benefited Eynsford poor; a cottage in Crockenhill was connected with this. Sir Percyvall Hart's grandfather also gave money for the poor, and he in 1635 gave £5 for the stocks! Tradesmen's tokens were used during the 17th century; a 1658 example of Eynsford grocer J.E.Becket was found at Horton Kirby. In 1659 Mrs Mary Bosvile 'a jewel taken out of a box, was shewn to the world and put up again, aged 17' (her memorial states), and in 1660 Sir Thomas Bosvile's widow 'put off her earthly tabernacle'.

Huguenots appear to have settled in Eynsford during the 17th century and were connected with the papermill operating by 1648. From 1601–50, there were only two papermills in Kent (Spilman's at Dartford and the Eynsford mill). At Horton Kirby in 1693 were married one Johannot and Margaret Fleurellon or Fleurendon, both of families connected with Eynsford mill. Thomas Burr, a weaver (1699) brought his trade from the Continent. By 1777 the mill was held by John Floyd, and in 1789 by Floyd and Fellows. John Wellard, paper maker of Eynsford, settled in Dartford and built the Zion Chapel in 1794. The corn-mill near the bridge, site of one of the Domesday mills, later became Walter Millen's bootlace factory and eventually moved to Horton Kirby.

Huguenots probably encouraged non-conformity in Eynsford. In 1658 and 1704 there are references to Anabaptists, and in 1792 Edward Hodges, who regularly walked to Wilmington Bible Meetings, encouraged John Morris, preacher from London, to come to Eynsford. The Baptist Church began in a stable in Priory Lane, moving in 1806 to the present site, where baptisms took place in the Darent, causing much local controversy.

Many large barns in Axstane can probably be dated to the 18th century at least, like one at Lower Austin Lodge Farm. Eynsford's 16th century bridge carried traffic from St Mary Cray and Crockenhill, and was repaired in 1710. There is a tradition that John Wesley preached here on his way to visit his friend Vincent Perronet, Vicar of Shoreham. In 1754 occurred the fire mentioned in the Brief at Sutton. A 1758 Inquiry found that there were 'no Papists', but oddly, 'no family of note'. The Rector of Lullingstone, Rev Davies Lambe, also held Ridley; not surprisingly, communion at Lullingstone was celebrated only five times annually! There was, at Eynsford 'no free school, no hospital, no almshouse'.

Lullingstone Castle exterior belies its earlier history; much of it is Tudor. The State Drawing Room has a decorative plaster barrel vault, with roundels representing Roman emperors. Two gatehouses were erected in 1497, the dovecote is of the same date, and there was a jousting ground. Sir John Peche's daughter Elizabeth married John Hart. Sir Percyval Hart, who succeeeded in 1545, was Chief Server and Knight Harbinger to four Tudor monarchs. The fine deer park originated in the 13th or 14th centuries, but declined during the turbulent 17th century.

Although in 1650 both Lullingstane and Lullingstone were described as parsonages the two parishes had merged in 1412.

The house was much altered in the 18th century, when another Percyval Hart inherited (1700). A new facade was added to the west front, and a pavilion at the south-east corner. New panelling was added to the State Drawing Room. Queen Anne visited on occasion. The cedars on the lawn may date from this time. When Percyval Hart died (1738) there came another change of dynasty, for his heiress daughter Anne married Sir Thomas Dyke of Horeham, Sussex. He gave the title 'castle' to the former house. His son, Sir John Dixon Dyke, demolished the inner gate-house, filled in the moat, removed the almshouses erected by Sir John Peche, and formed the lake, presumably part of his scheme of landscaping, which also included much replanting of trees and re-enclosing.

The Portobello Inn, West Kingsdown, may be earlier than 1713, date of the naval incident after which it is named. The earliest reference to the Cock (or Gamecock) is 1749. North of the Portobello stood Richardson's Farm; the Old Post Office building of the 17th century, may have been the farmhouse. The core of the house until 1967 east of the Portobello, known as the 'Manor House' though not so, was possibly a Wealden hall-house, but other evidence suggests the early 17th century. A glebe terrier refers to the Rector's house, still standing in 1853. Kingsdown Green seems by 1254 to have been a secondary nucleus of the village known as Dembre; the first reference to Kingsdown Green was in 1667, when Richard Coke consented to the erection of a poor house. Green Farm carried the name on in 1752. Many buildings in West Kingsdown were erected or altered in the 17th century, but Hever Place was a 15th or 16th century manor house built by the Lovelaces. It later became a tenanted farm, but in 1784 it passed to Duncan Campbell. Knockmill is another ancient site; in 1259 Henry atte Knocke is mentioned. Owners from before 1701 were the Polhills of Otford, leasing to the Wingates through the 18th century; one of the latter family owned the probably 17th century building later called Earlylands. Oaklands, later Cowgill's, appears in the late 18th century with Thomas Roffe or Rolfe as the first known owner. The present house is early 19th century. Knatts (1318 Le Gnat) was sold to Thomas Sybill of Farningham (1489); it later followed the Lovelace properties to Duncan Campbell.

Crowhurst Farm (c1450) was certainly a Wealden hall-house, subjected to later alterations. Henry le Crowe is recorded in 1272 but Thomas Crowe (will 1501) may have built it. It may have been part of Chepsted Manor. By the late 18th century the Hodsolls of South Ash held it.

Paganus de Bronkesheche, 1259, may well have been connected with Brands Hatch. Later it came to the Lovelaces, then to the Cokes. In 1667 Richard Whiffin occupied it and also rented Turner's Place, Ash, from Coke. Then came the Burrows from Hartley. In 1784 it too went to Duncan Campbell.

Pells (Pelle in 1545, when owned by Nicholas Sybill) is of uncertain origin. In 1675 Richard Goodhugh was occupier. The present house was built in the 18th century. Near Pells was the post mill demolished in 1909. The smock mill was erected nearby in 1880, after transfer from a site near the present Millfield Road, where it had stood in 1805. Both Old Terry's Lodge and Terry's Lodge itself are probably 18th century, and owned by William Evelyn of St Clere, Sheriff of Kent and a relative of John Evelyn the diarist, and later by Rev E.B.Evelyn. On the west side of the parish is East Hill Farm, dated 1672, with Richard Coke's initials on the chimney-stack. It too followed the familiar path from Lovelace to Coke and to Campbell.

The Manor of Woodlands is rather an anomaly. It was a separate ecclesiastical parish in the Hundred of Codsheath, and the church was in disrepair when, c1570, the parish was united with Wrotham. The Lovelaces and the Cokes held some of the Manor lands which overlapped into other parishes. It is now in West Kingsdown parish but, since 1975, has been ecclesiastically linked with Kemsing.

Ash church has a memorial to the learned Dr John Maxfield (died 1605). On the benefactions board is set out John Walter's will of 1623, which gave annually coats and gowns to the poorest two men and two women of each of the three parishes of Ash, Fawkham, and Hartley. After receiving the coats and gowns in church the recipients returned to Pennis for Christmas dinner. The clothing bequest carried on in that form until World War II.

In 1670–1 there was a rent charge on a house, later the King's Arms, closed c1844, in Hartley Bottom, near Cuckold's Corner. In 1702 Henry Johnson was blacksmith in the 'Borough' of Ash. Attwood Place was built in the early 18th century. Rev Samuel Attwood was Rector 1701–35, and left £20 for the establishing of a free school. Later James Trumbell was schoolmaster, and a Mr Waller Parish Clerk; they were succeeded in both posts by Richard Robson, who died in 1787. Attwood's successor, Dr John Pery, also Vicar of Farningham, rebuilt the Rectory (now the Old Rectory). A late 18th century Rector, Thomas Lambard, had the church re-floored and provided with tall pews c1792.

Between 1746 and 1782 many travellers passed this way, turning aside from the Maidstone and Gravesend roads for shelter. In 1769 an antiquarian visitor, John Thorpe, examined Scotgrove, remarking on what was believed to be the chapel site; even 40 years earlier no-one in the village recalled the name of the manor.

The Fulljames map of Ash (1792) shows Forge Pond south of Peasehill Road, no houses on Billet Hill, the 168 acre North Ash farm occupied by Tom Whittaker, while Thomas Waddow was at the forge near North Ash. The Royal Oak stood at West Yoke near Old House Farm. Hop garden field was next to Ash Place, and fields in Hartley Bottom were called 'Shooting Valleys'. Nicholas Hubble was at Berry's Maple Farm. The Green Man, Hodsoll Street, seems to have stood east, not west, of the Green; nearby was a house for the poor.

Although Fawkham Green lay in another parish, a fatal epidemic there in 1795 (probably typhoid) which killed seven, must have alarmed nearby Ash.

Ridley was 'little known and frequented' (said Hasted), but Courts Leet and Baron were held for its manor. Memorial slabs in the church to Rev John Lambe (d1740), and his son Davies Lambe, indicate how clergy often served more than one parish, even in times of limited travel. Both Rectors of Ridley, the father also served Longfield, the son Lullingstone.

Near Hartley church stood the tithe barn (like the barn, now the Oratory of St Francis de Sales, probably built in the 16th century), the stocks and whipping post. The Stokke (Stock Farm) was of the 15th and 16th centuries. The Manor House (c1650) later became Hartley Court.

Fairby (from Fereby or Feerby, a 15th century family) was built or rebuilt in 1612. During the 18th century it was held by the Youngs, but inherited by Richard Treadwell after his marriage to Mary Young, who died in 1792. This romance started with burglary and ended (or perhaps continues) with a ghost. The Bests were a yeoman family from Tudor times to 1883. John Best was Borsholder. Fereby, New House, and Middle Farms were the dominant farms during the 17th and 18th centuries. New House Farm (le Hayes in the 15th century) was held by the Overey family until the mid–17th century, and was rebuilt as New Hayes by one Burrows, probably in the 18th century. Middle Farm was held by Edward Best in the early 19th century. Red Cow Farm was reputedly a depôt for smugglers of lace and tobacco.

In 1687 the Rector (John Stacy) also held Ridley. Daniel Defoe is said to have lived in a cottage by the Black Lion. A poor house was on the opposite side. In 1746 a mounting block, symbol of a horse-owning society, was purchased, to be placed outside the Church. The first Parish Clerk known was William French (1747), while from 1779–1819 Francis Treadwell held the office.

Hasted describes Fawkham as 'a lonely, unfrequented place'. Away from the Fawkham Valley road it retains something of that character. It is a long, fairly narrow parish, bisected by the road. The original Manor House stood east of the Church; an inn may once have stood between Church and pond. Court Lodge incorporates a 14th century aisled hall, and very likely was the manor house for the second manor when Fawkham was first split in the late 13th century. Pennis House contains a fragment of Elizabethan Pennis, built by Thomas Walter as a new Manor House for

'Old' Fawkham. The house had three wings, a central court, and about 40 rooms and, like the earlier Franks Hall, Horton Kirby, represented a new age of prosperity. It was demolished, probably by fire, early in the 19th century. Thomas Walter married Alice Kettel of Darenth. Unusually, two daughters married successive Rectors of Ash (Dr Maxfield and William Baker). Thomas' son John is remembered for the 'coats and gowns' bequest; his wife Dorcas was sister to Samuel Michel, who married a Rudston of Horton Kirby. The Rector of Eynsford leased Eynsford Parsonage successively to his sons Thomas and George, the latter purchasing the Walter estates and moving to Pennis House. Later, Pennis went to John Selby, of the Ightham family.

The Cross House, near Pennis, where probably the village cross stood, has Elizabethan and Queen Anne period work. It was another building associated with 18th century smuggling activities. The old Rectory, though in appearance Georgian, was referred to in a terrier of 1634. Hook House (late White House) near Speed Gate, is Georgian. At Fawkham Green, the Rising Sun is probably late medieval. There was a Poor House at the Green until 1835. A constable and waywarden were appointed.

Longfield Hill had more houses than were around Longfield Church; it was as though some migration to higher ground had taken place. Mary Middleton, buried in the churchyard in 1530, may have been connected with Middleton Farm. Pinden, now in Longfield, was formerly in Horton Kirby, and there was a beer house on the Longfield–Dartford road east of the Pinden lane junction.

Hasted reported Southfleet as 'very isolated'; nearly 200 years later it retains that aspect.

Two early 17th century Rectors became important prelates. Richard Neile (1608–10) became Bishop of Rochester and Archbishop of York; John Buckeridge also took Rochester, followed by Ely. Elizeus Burgess (1628–42) became Archdeacon of Rochester but was ejected by Parliament. A note in the registers welcomes the Restoration: 'The persecution of the Church of England ends (God be praised) viz., ye restoring of King Charles ye Second his due rights at 29th May 1660'. Special prayers were inserted in the Prayer Book. In 1686 Elizabeth Ware, daughter of a shoemaker, took the King's Evil. Surveyors of Highways were appointed in 1704; the following year two Overseers for the Poor and two Borsholders were appointed, while in 1706 the number of Surveyors became four, and by 1762 the number of Overseers was also four. Five Briefs brought only 11s 2d. The name Colyer was now prominent and Edward Colyer (1714–88) of Mates Farm became churchwarden, while later, I. Colyer (died 1839) held Joyce Hall, Betsham.

Swanscombe still included Greenhithe, though the latter was always geographically separated, especially by the Ingress Abbey lands, and differentiated by its business as a small port. In 1634 it paid £13 7s 6d towards Ship Money, about half the amount paid by Dartford. Some benefactions, such as John Beer's three almshouses (1587) and Anthony Poulter's 20s to the poor (1635) were directly concerned with Greenhithe. Beer also ensured that Swanscombe had a right to send two boys to Dartford Grammar School.

During the Civil War Sir Anthony Weldon was Chairman of the County Committee under Parliament. It was said of him that, though he was faithful to Parliament, he was more so to Kent, and most of all to himself; but in a county with many Royalist sympathisers among the gentry he had no easy task. Nevertheless, while an able administrator, he was detested for his dictatorial manner, personal violence and spleen. His courage seems unquestioned. Combatting a rebellion against Parliament in 1643, supported by most of the gentry of the Darent Valley, including the Harts of Lullingstone, Sir Thomas Bosvile of Eynsford, and the Bathursts of Franks, he resolved to live and die with 30 men of his 'ragged regiment' at Dartford, where the Royalists seized the magazine. He later wrote to Parliament: 'God quenched the flame'. He was also involved before Canterbury in 1648, after the populace had been provoked into rebellion by the proscription of Christmas Day festivities, 1647. The Parliamentary gentry were concerned for sensible direction, and framed a petition to Parliament for lawful governance but, the County Committee forbidding this, a general rising took place. General Fairfax intervened, and at Stonebridge, by the Ebbsfleet near Swanscombe, there was a skirmish. Although Kent suffered no major action, the musters of men and the plundering of villages and hamlets for horses and waggons raised tempers in the county.

Another Anthony Weldon refused in 1660 to address Charles II on his Restoration. He was deprived of his Recordership of Rochester, and succeeded by Francis Barrell, father of a Vicar of Sutton.

But there were diversions: on 2 August 1652 three women from Swanscombe were tried as witches at Maidstone, and sentenced to death. About this time a stocks and pound existed by Swanscombe Church, and a lock-up near the London road. In 1661 occurred the murder at Gad's Hill near Shorne of Cassuma Albertus, Prince of Transylvania; the murderers – Hungarians – were traced to Greenhithe, where they had left their carriage at the King's Head (the White Hart).

Plans for a dockyard between Erith and Greenhithe lingered on until 1802 but came to nothing. Young people were indentured for employment well beyond Swanscombe's borders; in 1689 Anne Jefferyes and James Cole were bound to Richard Harris and Richard Clark, of Horton Kirby, presumably as servants.

The 18th century brought its share of Briefs; five in 1704 included one for 'widows and orphans whose husbands were swept away in the dreadful tempest 26/27 November 1703' (*ie* that which severely damaged Reynolds Place, Horton Kirby); in 1705 and 1708/9 fires in 'Inniskilling' (*sic*) in Ireland, and in the Canongate, Edinburgh brought financial help. In 1734, 'for loss sustained by inundation at Bibi Willar in the Valley of Lucerne in Piedmont' 15s 1d was raised; for an Eynsford fire in 1745 only 2s 3d could be found.

Among the Parish Officers of 1705 were two Churchwardens, two Overseers, two Borsholders and in 1706 three Surveyors (including Sir William Swan and Walker Weldon); by 1778, after turnpiking of the London road, there were eight Surveyors. By this time, Watling Street had deteriorated to no more than a footpath, and a variant of the Gravesend Road developed north of Swanscombe as Lower Road. By 1788 there was a ferry to Essex from Greenhithe. In 1772 there was a petition against gunpowder manufacture at Horton Kirby, for fear of danger in conveying the material to, and depositing at, Greenhithe.

The Mutiny at the Nore occurred in 1791 and Admiral Keppel presided at the Court Martial held on HMS *Standard*; the mutineers were put ashore at Greenhithe. The Admiral's name was long borne by the Pier Hotel.

Benefactions continued and, in 1721, Lady Swan gave land in Greenhithe High Street and also three messuages for the poor. A Poor's Acre had existed at least since 1680. In 1715 there was cattle disease and local cowkeepers were financially assisted.

Stone, despite the broad acres of its egg-timer shaped parish (with the tight neck on Watling Street), had a low population – probably only about 300, during the 17th–18th centuries.

Rector Richard Tillesley (1615–24) was James I's chaplain. In 1638 the Church had a disastrous fire, in which the chancel roof and windows were destroyed, and the bells melted as they hung. The Church's familiar description – 'Lantern of Kent' – since it overlooked the Thames and was a landmark for mariners, became reality. Rev Richard Chase restored it sufficiently for worship, but not sufficiently to offset, in Parliament's eyes, his family relationship with the Bishop of Rochester, and in 1650 he was removed. In 1662 a Puritan minister, John Price, was ejected. Two bells were replaced in 1676 and 1691; the first bears the name of Nicholas Tooke, Churchwarden (probably a son of Dartford iron mill owner Nicholas Tooke); the other, the gift of Henry Draper, shows that a Colyer was Churchwarden.

During the 18th century, as in Sutton, the Rector was often absent, in the case of Stone serving the Bishop, and the parish was served only by a curate. In 1718 only four baptisms were recorded, and until 1768 few years had more than ten. Burials in 1768–1812 were also few. In 1734 John Tasker of Dartford and Horton Kirby obtained land on Stone Marshes from Henry Pierce and in 1751 Stone House Farm was leased by Anne Edwards to J.Stadams. In 1776 the Parsonage (presumably the Old Rectory) had five lower rooms, six upper, a brewhouse and a coach house. The following year, in accordance with Georgian preferences, the Church nave was ceiled and a gallery built, and by 1778 five bells had been installed.

Between 1600 and 1700 the general population is believed to have increased by 15%. Assuming this rate continued to 1801 (first Census) the following figures result for the original Axstane area (including Wilmington, but excluding Dartford):

1600	4,700 (approx.)	(Dartford	1,900)
1700	5,400 (do.)	(Do.	2,170)
1801	6,173 (Census figure)	(Do.	2,498)

In 1801 the highest village populations were: Eynsford 841, Swanscombe (including Greenhithe) 763, Sutton-at-Hone 690. Tiny Lullingstone and Ridley had 33 and 47 respectively, while Longfield had only 99 people. Farningham, despite being sited on two turnpike roads had, at 397, less than half the population of Eynsford, while high (and dry) West Kingsdown had 337. Near neighbours Fawkham and Hartley ran virtually equal, with 149 and 151 respectively. Wilmington, close to Dartford, had 520, but Southfleet (508) and Ash (472) ran it close. Darenth and Stone, with their scattered hamlets and farms, made a matching pair – 407 and 403 respectively, while Horton Kirby had 356.

Long before the close of this period Dartford and Wilmington had been placed in a separate Hundred. The area outside Dartford was still virtually untouched by industry, but its major estates were increasingly held by the new gentry – London lawyers, businessmen, and officials. Despite – and in part perhaps because of – the Napoleonic Wars, coach traffic on the Dover and Maidstone roads was increasing. When 'Boney' should be conquered, the Industrial Revolution and speedier communications were poised to have marked effect on this rural enclave.

Lullingstone Castle on the occasion of a WI meeting in World Refugee Year 1960, to present a purse to Mr Christopher Chataway, Vice-Chairman of Refugee Year Committee. (KT/KCL DD)

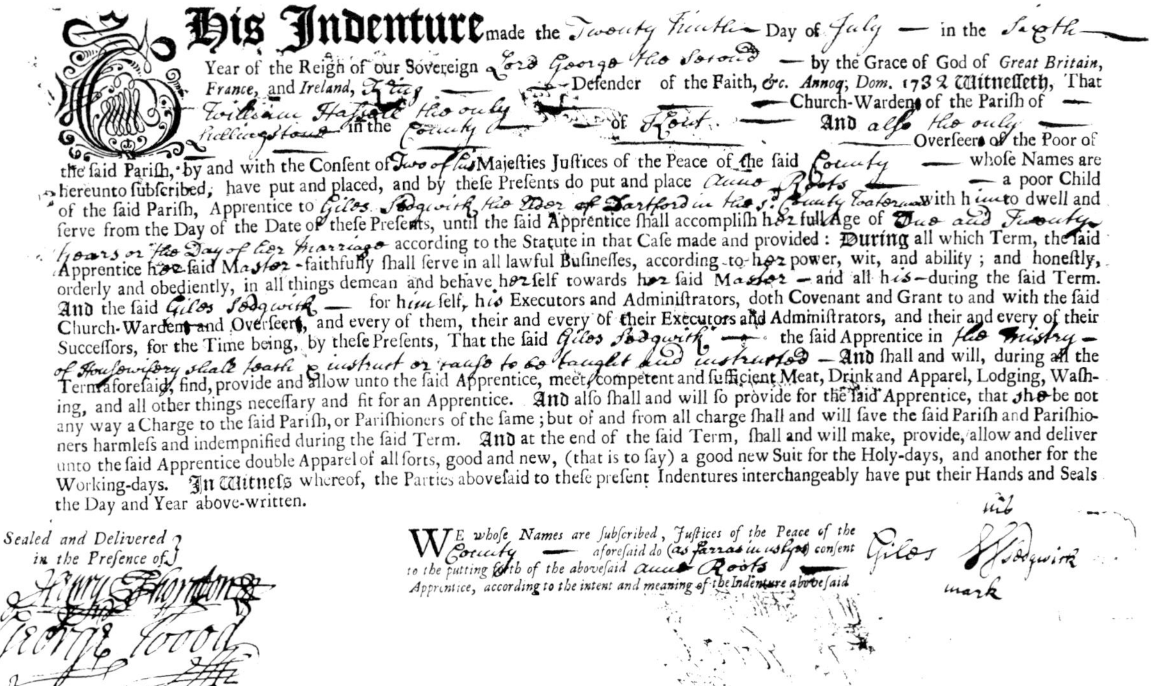

This Indenture made the Twenty Ninth Day of July — in the Sixth Year of the Reign of our Sovereign Lord George the Second — by the Grace of God of *Great Britain, France,* and *Ireland,* King — Defender of the Faith, *&c. Annoq; Dom.* 1732 Witnesseth, That William Hassell the only — Church-Wardens of the Parish of Lullingstone in the County of Kent. — And also the only — Overseers of the Poor of the said Parish, by and with the Consent of Two of His Majesties Justices of the Peace of the said County — whose Names are hereunto subscribed, have put and placed, and by these Presents do put and place Anne Roots — a poor Child of the said Parish, Apprentice to Giles Sedgwick the Elder of Dartford in the sd County Taylor with him to dwell and serve from the Day of the Date of these Presents, until the said Apprentice shall accomplish her full Age of One and Twenty Years or the Day of her Marriage according to the Statute in that Case made and provided: During all which Term, the said Apprentice her said Master faithfully shall serve in all lawful Businesses, according to her power, wit, and ability; and honestly, orderly and obediently, in all things demean and behave herself towards her said Master — and all his — during the said Term. And the said Giles Sedgwick — for himself, his Executors and Administrators, doth Covenant and Grant to and with the said Church-Wardens and Overseers, and every of them, their and every of their Executors and Administrators, and their and every of their Successors, for the Time being, by these Presents, That the said Giles Sedgwick — the said Apprentice in the Mistery of Housewifery shall teach & instruct or cause to be taught and instructed — And shall and will, during all the Term aforesaid, find, provide and allow unto the said Apprentice, meet, competent and sufficient Meat, Drink and Apparel, Lodging, Washing, and all other things necessary and fit for an Apprentice. And also shall and will so provide for the said Apprentice, that she be not any way a Charge to the said Parish, or Parishioners of the same; but of and from all charge shall and will save the said Parish and Parishioners harmless and indempnified during the said Term. And at the end of the said Term, shall and will make, provide, allow and deliver unto the said Apprentice double Apparel of all sorts, good and new, (that is to say) a good new Suit for the Holy-days, and another for the Working-days. In Witness whereof, the Parties abovesaid to these present Indentures interchangeably have put their Hands and Seals the Day and Year above-written.

Sealed and Delivered in the Presence of
Henry Thornton
George Wood

WE whose Names are subscribed, Justices of the Peace of the County — *aforesaid do* (as far as in us lyes) *consent to the putting forth of the abovesaid* Anne Roots *Apprentice, according to the intent and meaning of the Indenture abovesaid*

Giles his GS mark Sedgwick

LEFT: Manor House Farm, Swanscombe, since demolished. (ED) RIGHT: Reynold's Place, Horton Kirby, c1900. Mr Tom Aldworth, Brewer of Dartford, who lived there, is on extreme right. (He was partner to Richard Coomb Miller of Oakfield Park, Wilmington). BELOW: Apprenticeship Indenture: Ann Roots of Lullingstone to be apprenticed to Giles Sedgwick the Elder of Dartford, to be instructed in housewifery, 1732. (Both KCL/DD)

ABOVE: Ingress Abbey, Greenhithe and the village in 1752. (KCL/DD)
LEFT: Edward Hasted (1732–1812) author of *A History and Topographical Survey of Kent*, who lived at St John's Jerusalem during the 18th century. (BL)
RIGHT: The White House, Farningham; built shortly before Hasted wrote his *History*. (MJ)

ABOVE: Lion Hotel, Farningham. (KCL DD) BELOW: St John's Jerusalem, (with Mr John Russell), c1900; formerly the Commandery Church of the Knights Hospitallers. (KCL DD)

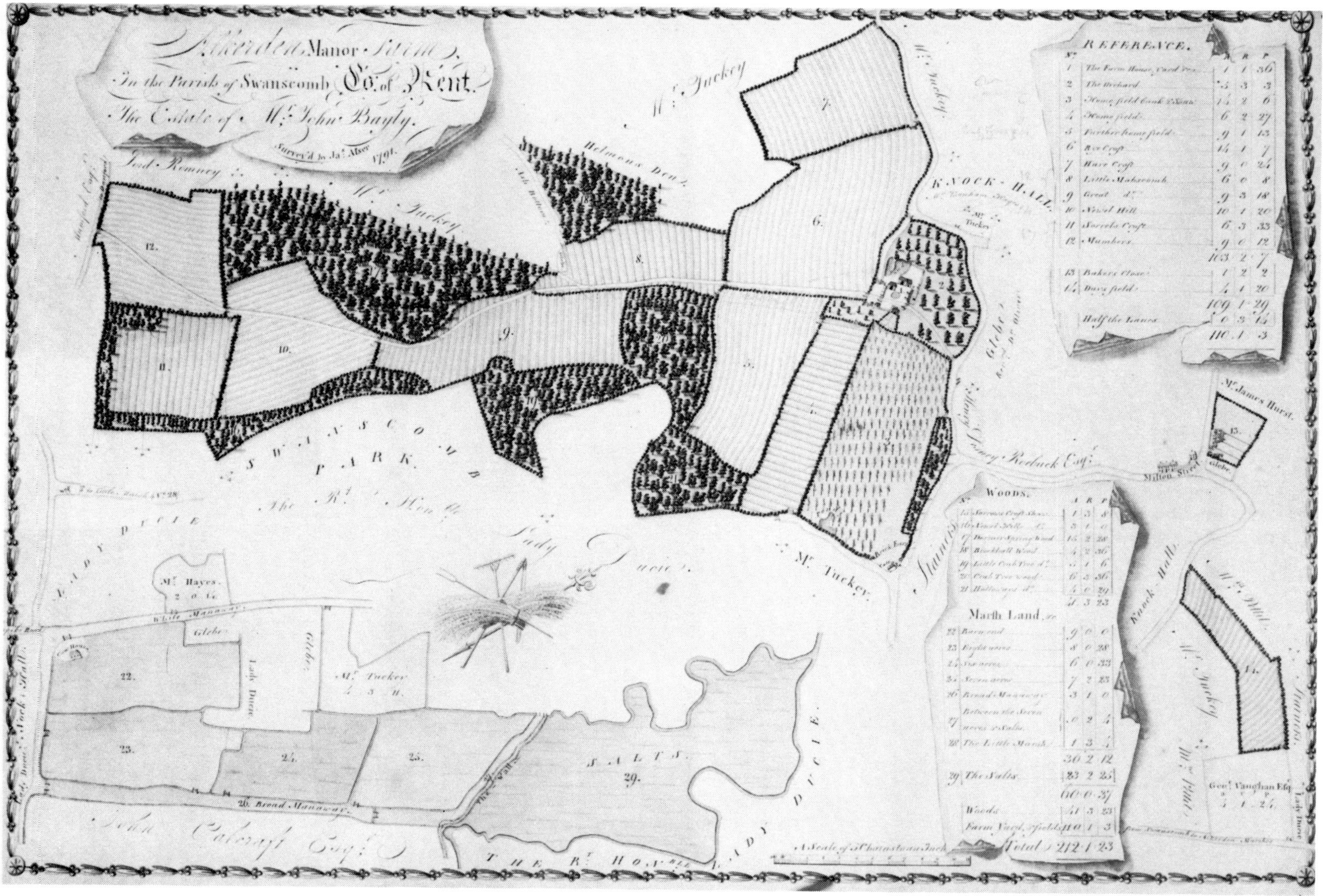

Estate map of the Manor of Alkerden (Coombs) 1791, then held by Mr John Bayly. (KCAO)

Tilling the Soil

Until the 19th century, Axstane saw little manufacturing or extractive industry, and the majority of the rural population had been dependent upon the land. The expansion of London between the 17th and 19th centuries ensured a demand for grain from North Kent, while the introduction of foreign grasses such as saintfoil and white clover after the Restoration aided the feeding of cattle and sheep. No longer was the wholesale slaughter of cattle in autumn necessary, for meal could be stored for their sustenance. While eight–ox teams were still working during the 18th century, by 1700 less oxen were used. Prosperity brought increased horse-ownership, towards which the general introduction of lucerne (from Holland c1750) for meal was a response.

Anthony Roper's engrossment and destruction of several farms around Farningham was perhaps exceptional, and he was severely criticised, but his action demonstrated the influence of the nearby conurbation – the need for arable land making for larger farming estates. Perhaps he was before his time. Hop and fruit-growing were developing too and, although costly and calling for extra-seasonal labour, they enabled farmers to diversify and specialise in crops requiring less acreage than corn. Axstane has remained mainly arable partly because of its soil, and there has been little dairying.

During the 17th century the proportion of wheat produced in North Kent was significantly reduced, while oats tripled, and the production of beans and peas greatly increased between 1680 and 1700. But the corn market at Dartford remained important.

Despite problems induced by the Civil War there was generally a growing stability. Yeomen continued to prosper and labourers enjoyed higher wages than elsewhere. Between 1600 and 1700 the daily wage (fixed at Quarter Sessions) rose from 1s to 1s 3d. Labour was long – 4 am to 8 pm (or 10 pm in summer). The drudgery of life was to some extent mitigated by locally brewed beer (Wilmington and Stone eventually had breweries), often used as part-payment of wages. And there were of course the harvest festivities. In 1642, when Orkesden (Austin Lodge, Eynsford) was owned by the Lennard family (well-known at Chevening), it was leased to ten tenants. In 1651 woods at Southfleet and Ridley were among those providing timber for the Navy. Timber was also required for firing for London – and, of a different type, hops required poles. After the Fire of London, bricks were increasingly required for new building, and in time each village would have its brickfield. Chalk, already extracted and transported from Greenhithe to Essex, was increasingly used for marling the soil, and John Banister of Horton Kirby (*Synopsis of Husbandry*, 1799) describes the digging of chalk wells for this purpose; 80 to 100 loads (12 bushels to one load) were required per acre. The flinty nature of much downland ensured, together with increased horse-shoeing and waggon and carriage repairing, a living for village blacksmiths. Pigeon houses became more plentiful. Although cottages remained humble, with but two or three rooms and furnishings of £5–6 value, the rural standard of living was increasing. Nevertheless the general status of North Kent was middling. None of the greatest county gentry, with annual income exceeding £3,000, lived here. Compared with them, the Harts of Lullingstone, with £900 had 'a moderate estate, not wasted by luxury nor increased by Avarice'. During the 17th century their great deer park had declined, but in the 18th, Sir Thomas Dyke and his son Sir John Dixon Dyke made many improvements.

There were of course many other factors influencing the farmer. Inevitably the weather was one. Banister records the five weeks and one day's frost from 23 December 1762 to 28 January 1763. He writes of the 'prolific harvest' of 1779 (though with war preventing export, the price of wheat sank from 52s a quarter to 32s). With a low crop in 1780 the price rose and the 5½d (2¼p) quartern loaf became 7¼d (3p). That year the effect of the American War of Independence was felt on hops – demand lessened and the price dropped. In 1782, with a moist spring and the coldest summer Banister could remember, hops failed and flour was commercially damaged, bread was 'cludgy' (lovely word!) and pastry ill-tasted. Two years later the harvest was the wettest he could recall. Another consideration in hop production (said Banister) was the buying and selling by factors, or the holding back of hops from market, both to keep up prices; another, the frequent destruction of the fragile bines; and yet another, the type of labour required, for good wages attracted men unaccustomed to particular types of work. But old John was no less critical of English workers than he was of the many Irish he apparently encountered, reminding employers of the 'knavery and tricks of servants', which led (for instance) to the lack of care for horses. For fruit-picking, women were preferred because of their nimbler fingers. Paupers and children were often employed. For haymaking, two people per acre were required.

Banister was a great believer in the dung-cart, including material from the farmer's own yard. There would be increasing supplies coming from London streets, hauled from Dartford Creek or Greenhithe.

The Tithe Awards and Maps stemming from the Tithe Commutation Act 1836 portray land ownership and occupancy about 1840. Monastic land had been exempt from Tithe, and the lands in Sutton formerly belonging to the Knights Hospitallers, and in 1840 held by Mumford Campbell, were still exempted. (Including lands held by Ann Mumford and Rev John Egerton in Hextable, 607 acres were exempt). Much of this land was around the former Commandery; off Ship Lane; Hollow Deanes (near Clement Street) and the Lord's Goss. This relaxation does not appear to have applied to St John's, Ash. The Tithe Awards also show, in the cases of the northern parishes of Axstane, the basis of agricultural production prior to the introduction of other types of industry.

Arable land dominates the scene by far – six times the area of meadow and pasture, four times the woodland. The main arable crops were oats, barley and wheat, in that order in every parish. Three parishes had over 2,000 acres of arable: Eynsford (2,668), Sutton (2,435), Horton Kirby (2,077). Production was in inverse order: Horton Kirby (6,622 bushels, total), Sutton (5,497), and Eynsford (5,468), a sequence repeated for the individual crops. The value of fruit and hops cannot of course be judged by mere acreage, but of a total acreage of about 34,000 (including 23,000 arable) 855 acres were devoted to fruit and 582 to hops. As might be expected, Wilmington and Sutton had most orchard acreage and, with Eynsford and Southfleet, had nearly three-quarters of the fruit acreage. The downland parishes from West Kingsdown to Longfield had miniscule fruit acreages. Ash had by far the greatest acreage under hops (169¼), the nearest to approach that being Southfleet (only 67½) and West Kingsdown (61¼). Even little Ridley had 28¾ acres, more than Stone, four times its size. Darenth had 46 acres, Horton Kirby 43, but neighbouring Sutton recorded no hop-gardens. The only others with nil acreages were Lullingstone (mainly parkland) and Eynsford (either high exposed downland or narrow valley with meadows). There were increased Tithe rent charges for acreages under fruit and hops.

A comparison may be made between two villages of approximately equal size, one in the Darent Valley (Eynsford) the other on downland (Ash); a second Valley village (Sutton-at-Hone) confirms the Eynsford figures.

Eynsford		Ash	Sutton
2,668	Arable	1,780	2,435
75	Pasture	180	337
121	Fruit	–	155
–	Hops	169	–
482	Woodland	625	408
3,346 (Acres)		2,999*	3,335

* includes 245 acres described as 'worn out cinquefoil [saintfoil] land'.

Note that Sutton possesses a wider area of pasture on its generally lower ground beyond the Valley, than the other two.

As will be seen, the most striking differences are the lower acreage of arable in Ash and the choice of fruit over hops in the Valley villages (which are also nearer London).

Between a downland and a Thames-side village of approximately equal size (West Kingsdown and Stone) there are expected differences.

West Kingsdown		Stone
1,500	Arable	1,730
295	Pasture	526
7	Fruit	72
61	Hops	26
787	Woodland	454
2,700	(Acres)	2,808

The greater extent of woodland in the hilly downland parish is offset by the increased marshland pasturage of Stone as well as the larger arable acreage.

Land ownership in general was in the hands of the few, although much of it was worked by tenants. Apart from Lullingstone and Eynsford, where almost all the land was owned by the Hart Dyke family, and Ridley, where one owner (William Lambard) held two-thirds of the land – as well as a third of Ash – in most parishes four landowners held two-thirds of the land.

Land-ownership was not of course confined within parish boundaries. Within Axstane the Hart Dykes owned land in Sutton and Farningham as well as in the two parishes mentioned above – 5,243 acres in Axstane alone. Mumford Campbell and his relations held 3,197 acres, including 1,721 in Sutton and W.N.Campbell's 1,047 acres in West Kingsdown. J. Clark Powell held 1,104 acres in West Kingsdown, 483 in Horton Kirby, 246 in Farningham, and other pieces to total 1,858 acres. The several Colyers held 1,704 acres, mainly in Southfleet, Stone, and Farningham, while William Lambard held 1,120 acres in Ash and Ridley. The Dean and Chapter of Rochester held 725 acres (479 in Darenth, and smaller areas in Wilmington, Sutton, Southfleet and Stone). Villiers in Swanscombe held 710 acres, and others, included the brewing family of Fleet, who held over 400 acres, mainly in Darenth.

But farmers also amassed large acreages. Among the best known was the family of Solomon, who together farmed 2,251 acres (1,538 of which were rented) in Dartford, Darenth, Stone, Swanscombe and West Kingsdown. Jeremiah Solomon worked five farms in Dartford and Stone, and Mrs Mary Solomon worked Maplescombe. James Russell, whose signature appears as Surveyor or Valuer on many Tithe Awards, held 426 acres plus 1,529 rented, in Horton Kirby, Farningham, Fawkham and West Kingsdown. (The Horton Kirby land included the 404 acre Court Lodge Farm still owned by Queen's College, Oxford). George Russell held 79 acres in Wilmington (he lived at Wilmington Hall) and W.E.Russell 505 acres (500 rented!) in

Swanscombe. The Ray family, based on Reynold's Place, Horton Kirby held 867 acres in Horton, Farningham and Eynsford, and occupied a further 517 acres (total 1,384). The name Andrus ran, not only through Southfleet, but in eight other parishes, with an interest in 1,112 acres.

These combined ownerships and rentals meant that many farms in several parishes came under single control; farm management of this kind is no modern phenomenon. Thus James Russell worked, in addition to Court Lodge Farm, Horton Kirby, Speedgate Farm, South Darenth Farm, Dean Bottom, Brands Hatch and Little Brands Hatch, and Charton Farm, Farningham.

Other farmers, like Tom Waring, held but one farm (in his case White Hill Farm at Farningham), or simply rented a farm (as Tom Phillips at Wested, from Sir Percival Hart Dyke). Some farms were little more than smallholdings; Fisher's House Farm in Hodsoll Street, Ash, was only eight acres – including 5¼ acres arable, and ½ acre each of orchard and pasture.

Jeremiah Solomon was influential in founding the Dartford Cattle Market c1840; this continued for about 120 years. Dartford Farmers' Club was founded soon after 1840, the Farningham and Dartford Agricultural Association started in 1852 and in 1879 its far-famed successor, the North Kent Agricultural Association, which ran the great annual ploughing matches in the district.

Ash, with nine other parishes on its boundaries, was perhaps exceptional in having twenty farms or parts of farms on and overlapping its territory. Within Farningham's boundaries were lands of thirteen farms, six based within the parish.

Field names reflect the past, and the Tithe Awards give these. Most villages once had vineyards, and the name remained at Wilmington, Sutton (Swanley), Horton Kirby, Ash, and elsewhere, and even Upper and Lower Vines at Swanscombe suggest this origin. Pigeon House Field is frequently found, and the Lints (Wilmington) or Lintzes (Swanscombe) suggest the growing of flax. Most villages have a Broomfield or Broomhill, some a Goss (Sutton for instance), and Chalkhole Fields are frequently found. Brickyard Field (Wilmington) and Brick Kiln Wood (Darenth) are examples of extensive brickmaking. Manifold are the 'Shaws' – narrow strips of woodland, usually serving as windbreaks or boundaries, among them Oliver's Shaw in Eynsford. The term Haw at Eynsford (mentioned more than once there, but uniquely in Axstane) usually refers to enclosed land near a house.

Other names have more curious interest, such as Devil's Dale, Hanging Oxendown and Lark's Spring, all among the Court Lodge lands at Horton Kirby. The second may suggest a gibbet of the distant past. Gazing Star Field in Southfleet is even more intriguing. Others give archaeological clues, such as Chapel Field near St Margaret Helles, and another, similarly named, west of Eglantine Lane, Farningham; there were chapels at both sites.

The Tithe Maps tell further detail, such as where many ponds were. For instance, one lay within the road-fork near the Ship at Green Street Green; another was in the green triangle at Longfield Hill; two were in High Road, Wilmington until quite recent times. Ridley, its remoteness giving it little reason to infill them, still has several.

Queen Victoria was now on the throne, and the Great Exhibition would be held in a few years' time. In an industrial sense, that signalled a new age, although the Industrial Revolution had long since begun. Many still living and who remember speaking with people who could recall Victoria's accession and the Great Exhibition, must surely appreciate the brevity of that time – yet how much has been packed into it, even in Axstane.

ABOVE: A Kent waggon (example at Meopham), from an illustration by Tom Hennell (1903–45), son of the Rector of Ash-cum- Ridley, (reproduced from his book *Change in the Farm* by courtesy of Cambridge University Press). (MJ) BELOW: Haymaking in Dartford country.

ABOVE: Corner of a hop garden, (KCL DD) and BELOW: the old mill Darenth, c1910. (KCL DD)

ABOVE: The Mill and Mill House, Farningham, 1984, (MJ) and BELOW: Shire Hall Farm, Wilmington (16th century), c1910 — demolished in 1912. (ECY/KCL DD)

ABOVE: Farningham Fair, c1920. BELOW: Wicker-work arch constructed by Tom Moody, basket-maker of Swanley, in honour of the Prince of Wales' (later Edward VII) first visit, probably to open one of the Homes. (Both KCL DD)

ABOVE: Corn threshing at Crockenhill c1860. (GG/KCL DD) CENTRE: 19th century farm machinery demonstrated near Farningham, c1862: an illustration which first appeared in the *Illustrated London News* that year). (KCL DD) BELOW: Spring Cabbage at Middleton Farm, Longfield c1900. (DGR)

ABOVE: A party of Horton Kirby hop-pickers (Mrs Flewin on the right, middle row), c1920, and LEFT: Mrs Chapman of Horton Kirby and her family, hop-picking c1920. (Both PF) RIGHT: West Kingsdown Windmill. (MC)

ABOVE: Watercress beds at South Darenth c1905. (KCL DD) BELOW: Eynsford Badger Club c1930, including Major Henderson, and Stan and Arthur Rivers. (KR)

ABOVE: Eynsford: the Bridge, c1900. (KCL DD) LEFT: Mr F. Crouch and his grapes, grown in Eynsford 1960. (KT/KCL DD) RIGHT: For evenings after labour: interior of an Eynsford cottage next to the Plough (now demolished). (KCL DD)

Axstane's Variety

London's population rose six-fold between 1801 and 1901; Axstane's rose only five-fold because of rural decline. Ash-cum-Ridley's population rose by little more than 25%, West Kingsdown's increase was only 50%, Fawkham and Hartley failed to double theirs, while Southfleet's little more than doubled. But Wilmington's rose nearly fourfold, and Sutton's nearly sevenfold, both affected by local industry (including market gardening) and the attraction of London train services. Industrialised Swanscombe and part-industrialised Stone had nine and twelve-fold increases respectively!

The major increase came in the latter half of the century. Between 1801 and 1851, Axstane's population increased only by 2/3rds; between 1851 and 1901, nearly three times.

Improvements in communications aided industrial development. Even in turnpike days traffic was rapidly increasing. The railway through Dartford opened in 1849. Proposals for a Dartford–Sevenoaks line failed, but the London, Chatham and Dover Company opened the Rochester line in 1860, and their Sevenoaks line through Eynsford in 1862.

Dartford Creek was heavily used. In 1835 a Bill proposing a 'Dartford and Crayford Ship Canal and Kent and Essex Ferry' was defeated, and a lesser scheme (c1840) for straightening the Creek was only partially completed, but both emphasise that use. Pike and Edsell's powder mill of 1732 in Wilmington used the Creek for despatching gunpowder, while horse-dung from London streets was imported for manuring farmland. Their conveyance through Dartford offended the townsfolk, and in 1874 a steam tramway from the Creek to Farningham was proposed: the 'Dung and Gunpowder Railway'. An ambitious scheme was the 'London and Tilbury, and Dartford and Kent Coast Railway' (1876), with a tunnel to Stone, connecting with the three lines running through Axstane, a new Thames-side wharf, and Dartford wharf; and in 1897 a light railway from Dartford to Eynsford, with branches from Farningham to Vigo (climbing 600 feet) and to Swanley, was proposed. These proposals came to nothing. In 1902 the slogan 'Ocean wharves for Dartford' first appeared – 80 years before its time.

A horse-bus ran from Dartford to Farningham in the 1830s. In 1866 Holland's *Vivid* and *Wonder* took 70 minutes to Eynsford. A motorbus route to Sevenoaks was eventually adopted by the London General Company, while in 1921 route 21A commenced its first London journey from Farningham. That year the East Surrey Traction Co commenced its Dartford–Crockenhill 407 (now 477) route, and route 423 to Birchwood was extended to Swanley Junction in 1931. After World War II the latter was extended to West Kingsdown, and the Dartford terminal was later extended to Longfield, and eventually to New Ash Green. The Dartford–Gravesend 'North Kent' service began in 1913 and later operated by the Maidstone and District Motor Services Ltd, was taken over with the other services by the London Passenger Transport Board on its formation in 1933. A London service was established on this road in 1928 and became a Green Line route. Another Green Line route from Farningham across London was extended to Wrotham in 1933, but was abandoned in recent years.

Dartford Council Tramways commenced operation in 1906, their eastern terminus being at Horn's Cross (Stone), with a spur to the Orange Tree, Wilmington. Gravesend Tramways terminated at Swanscombe, railway opposition preventing a link-up. (After the Dartford trams' destruction by fire in 1917, Bexley Council Tramways took over until 1935. The succeeding trolley-bus and 'bus services terminated at Dartford.)

Darenth Hire Services ran into Dartford during the 1930s, and Thames Weald's Sevenoaks–Romford route serves outlying Axstane areas. Ash, Southfleet and central Swanscombe services link them with Gravesend.

In 1797 HMS *Neptune* requested a postal service for Greenhithe, and a letter-carrier was appointed to walk from Dartford; in 1867 William Saxby used a donkey-cart. The villages complained of the lack of a good postal service, the Post Office replying that the Penny Post generated insufficient revenue.

Trunk Roads A2 and A20 opened 1923–4. Now M25 crosses Axstane to Dartford Tunnel and M20 parallels A20.

Stone, Greenhithe and Swanscombe became the home of the Kent cement industry. Portland Cement was patented by Joseph Aspdin in 1824. In 1837 John Bazley White built Swanscombe Works, making 'Roman' and 'British' cement. His works manager, I.C.Johnson, had by 1844 discovered the principles of Portland Cement and, by 1862, White employed 750 men, producing 30,000 tons annually out of 200,000 tons country-wide. Johnson built his own works, opened in 1877 with 300 employees. By 1900 the chalk estate covered 200 acres. Eventually clay for slurry came from the Company's lands at Bean. During the late 19th century three works were erected on the Stone Court estate and two more at Greenhithe. Stone's little brewery seemed justified.

In 1900 the Associated Portland Cement Manufacturers (1900) Ltd was formed, and by 1911 owned 75% of the industry. The Kent Portland Cement Co commenced c1920 and was absorbed by APCM. In 1926 APCM had 126 sailing barges. By 1970 both Johnson's and Kent Works were closed. Swanscombe Works alone remains. In 1978 the trade name 'Blue Circle' was adopted.

Gravel was also quarried, and the Thames Sand Dredging Co was established. West of Kent Works were a whiting works, the Stone Court Ballast Co, and the concrete producing Atlas Stone Co, (closed 1975). In 1939 Littlebrook Power Station commenced operations; Littlebrook 'D' has lately commenced.

A plan for siting a Naval Arsenal between Greenhithe and Northfleet in 1805 failed. In 1880 the shipbuilding firm of F.T.Everard & Sons Ltd was founded; the repair yard closed in 1982. In 1908 the Wallpaper Manufacturers moved into Greenhithe, their mill later becoming the Empire Paper Mills Ltd (acquired in 1952 by the Reed Paper Group).

Between Swanscombe and Northfleet were the British Vegetable Parchment Mills and British Plaster Board Ltd. In Bean in 1891 was established the EC Powder Works (closed c1928).

In the Darent Valley at Eynsford, the 17th century papermill was owned by 1900 by Arnold and Foster. The mill closed in 1952 but was later used for manufacturing vulcanised fibre by Spaulding Russell Ltd until finally closing in 1981. The site is now being developed for housing. The bridge flour mill was held early this century by Walter Miller for manufacturing shoe-laces. In 1914 he transferred the business to the former flour mill in Horton Kirby. That, the Westminster Mill, was later owned by J. Day & Co Ltd, and suffered two serious fires in 1974 and 1975.

Horton Kirby Paper Mills was established on the site of one of South Darenth's two flour mills. Spalding and Hodge, and (1820–1843) John Hall were connected with it. Later it produced quality paper for *The Graphic*. By 1885 the mill had attained its full size, with its noteworthy 175ft chimney (to which was added a further 50ft). During this century the mill was taken over by the Reed Paper Group, then by the Inveresk Group, and was eventually bought by Nash (Foots Cray). Some wallpaper is produced there, but part of the site is used for other industry and housing.

The small Darent Valley Gas Works was in South Darenth.

Darenth and Hawley Mills were owned during the mid–19th century by T.H.Saunders of the Phoenix Paper Mills, Dartford. Handmade paper was produced at Darenth until 1931; the Darenth Fabric Printing Co was established there in 1939. Hawley Mill continued until c1917 (and led to further housing in that area). Later Bevingtons & Sons, leather manufacturers, took over, and the mill is now occupied by Graham Ford, builders' merchants.

Agriculture continued to predominate however, even though the import of American wheat during the 1870s helped cause the closure of South Darenth, Farningham and Eynsford flour mills by 1900. Fruit-growing, relatively unimportant in 1800, became a major industry by 1900 in response to the London demand for jam. In 1819 tariffs had encouraged increased production; better communications brought costs down, while sugar prices were also lower. In 1845 strawberries were grown at Springhead Gardens, which was rapidly becoming a pleasure spot. After 1878 depression in hop markets persuaded more farmers to try fruit-growing, and by 1900 Wilmington, Sutton, Swanley and Crockenhill formed the centre of the soft-fruit industry in the British Isles, while orchards were also established at Southfleet and Bean.

Since 1805 Springhead had been well-known for watercress, and in 1936 it was still grown there. It was also grown in the Darent Valley at Horton Kirby, Sutton and Darenth.

The fruit-pickers' huts were often insanitary and Arthur Mee, editor of the *Children's Newspaper* and *Encyclopaedia*, who lived in Hextable, was a prominent protestor over their living conditions.

A Horticultural College was established in the midst of this activity. After the Egerton Hextable estate broke up c1876 A.H.Bond bought Hextable House for horticultural experiments. This became a mixed college in 1891, but in 1902 an important college for the technical training of women. In 1915 Queen Mary visited the College and, under Dr Kate Barrett CBE (Principal 1916–44), the work greatly expanded. In 1945 the College was linked with the South-East Area College to form Wye College (London University). The mansion house, with its hall formed from the saloon of ss *Bessemer* by a previous resident, Sir Edward Reed, Founder-secretary of the Institute of Naval Architects, was demolished.

Agriculture requires machinery. During the 1850s the Dray family of Farningham demonstrated new machinery, including (1857) Le Play's Patent Beet Root Distillery. Such demonstrations were often given at Ploughing Matches. G.J.Garrett & Sons Ltd (Sutton-at-Hone), was founded in 1881; an early patent was the 'Garrett' expanding horse-hoe. (Their successors are Ernest Doe & Sons Ltd). In the mid-19th century 20,000 sheep and 1,000 tons of hops were exported annually from the Valley while, during the 1920s, cattle were still being driven to market through Dartford streets. In 1855 the first (week-long!) exhibition of poultry, of 'a national character', was held in Farningham, where also the Cattle Shows and annual Horse Fair continued.

Under the Poor Law Amendment Act of 1834, all the village workhouses were absorbed into the enlarged Dartford Union Workhouse, administered by a Board of Guardians. Village workhouses were sold and contributions made to the Union Workhouse. This new organisation relieved Parish Vestries of an onerous responsibility, but other responsibilities developed. Extension of burial grounds became urgent. At Wilmington, several extensions are recorded, and at Swanscombe a large area opposite the Church was used. Another essential service was water; Stone had to wait until 1878 for the Kent Waterworks Co to instal a mains supply. West Kingsdown, high on the North Downs, had to wait until 1910, and until 1937 for electricity; it still awaits mains gas. Stone received its electricity from the Kent Electric Power Co in the 1920s but Bean, only three miles from Dartford, had to wait until 1947. Main drainage and sewerage systems were long in reaching the villages – Dartford's own system was not completed until long after 1875, and the town protested against its marshes having to receive the Darent Valley main sewer.

Remote places continued with their dry closets and cesspools. West Kingsdown was connected to main drainage only in 1968.

Southfleet school, founded 1637, claims to be the oldest primary school in the country; other villages waited over 200 years for similar establishments. Sutton's dame school charged 6d weekly, which few parents could afford, and Rev J.H.Hotham (Vicar 1836–80) started a school adjoining the Wrote Almshouses. Later, with assistance from the National Society, he built Sutton Schools (replaced 1963). He also formed a village library. Swanley received a school as a condition of a church being authorised; it opened in 1862. Wilmington school was erected in 1850, but has been superseded. Horton Kirby had a dame school, but a parochial school in 1860; a new school, near South Darenth, was erected in 1894. At the Homes for Little Boys, homeless and destitute London lads were educated and taught trades. The foundation stone was laid by Princess (later Queen) Alexandra in 1866. Social changes eventually rendered the Homes impracticable and they closed in 1961. Similar homes, for fatherless boys, were opened in Hextable in 1883 by the Prince and Princess of Wales, and in 1907 Sir Christopher (later Lord) Furness endowed a house for training boys for the Mercantile Marine. These Homes closed in 1956, the buildings becoming a school for retarded children.

In Farningham two day schools existed in 1807. The Vicar, Rev W. Van Mildert (later Bishop of Durham) founded a Sunday School by 1811; one of the subscribers was Vice-Admiral Bligh (formerly of the *Bounty*), who lived in the Manor House. A new building erected on glebe land in 1823 became the National School, but failed to meet the standards of the 1870 Act, and in 1873 a new one was opened in Horton Way. Farningham's private schools included one run by John Rogers, Eynsford's Baptist Minister; Richard Whiffin's 'Gentleman's Boarding Academy' (1819–36), and Mrs Lockyer's 'Ladies' Boarding School'.

In conjunction with Eynsford Baptist Chapel, a British School was opened in Eynsford c1843. Mary Ann Hearn who, as Mary Ann Farningham, became famous as hymn-writer and editor, attended this school from her Farningham home. It became a Board School in 1892. The National School was rebuilt in 1905 in Bower Lane. The present Anthony Roper School caters for Farningham and Eynsford children.

Ash had a girls' school (now a nursery school), in 1839; a boys' school seems to have been near the White Swan. In Hartley, one of the Black Lion cottages was a school, but in 1841 a new one was erected on the Green 'for the children of the labouring, manufacturing and poorer classes' of Hartley, Fawkham and Longfield. By 1873 Fawkham had a National School.

West Kingsdown's Rector Thomas Willis (1794–1800) educated six children a year. There was a dame school and a school was built at Woodlands in 1851. The National School opened in 1874.

Swanscombe had a British School on Galley Hill, a National School (1844) and an Infants' School in Swanscombe Street. At Greenhithe in 1873 a day school was being considered. Stone's National School opened in 1866 on the main road north of Stone Castle; later one was built near the church, itself now superseded. In London Road began Brent School. Bean had a school in 1894. Darenth had a Sunday School building in 1839 and later a school on the Green Street Green road.

In 1863 the Dartford Highways Board and in 1872 the Dartford Rural Sanitary Authority took over those responsibilities from parish vestries, and these two organisations formed the basis for the Rural District Council established under the Local Government Act, 1894. (Swanscombe became an Urban District). Parish Councils were also established, leaving the Vestries only the function of appointing Churchwardens. Later, for specifically church affairs, the Enabling Act of 1919 authorised Parochial Church Councils. The County Council, founded under the Local Government Act, 1888, took over responsibilities for Police, Fire Brigades, Weights and Measures, and (in 1902) Education. The Board of Guardians' duties were transferred under another Local

Government Act (1929); a notable Chairman was Rev Stanley Morgan, Greenhithe's Congregational Minister earlier in the 20th century.

In 1974 Axstane underwent only its second major partition since Saxon times (the first was the creation of the Hundred of Dartford and Wilmington) when on 1 April 1974 the Rural District was split betweeen the new Sevenoaks and Dartford Districts (the latter forming a new Borough in 1977). Seven villages only remained with Dartford (if one may with respect so include Swanscombe/Greenhithe, now under a Town Council).

Before these developments however, the separate identity of Swanley village had long been recognised in Sutton. Rev J.H.Hotham foresaw the need for a separate church and parish, and these were achieved in 1861 and 1862. Meanwhile Hextable had only three houses, but the Egerton estate sale after 1876 led to speculative building of high-class villas. These plans were only partially successful, but the Rollo estate and development south of Top Dartford Road began. Later, plans existed for development (including an hotel!) west of Goss Hill, but this lapsed. After 1950, Council and other housing was erected off Swanley Bottom Road (Fenn's Farm).

There were also only three houses on the site of the future town of Swanley, near the junction station between the Rochester and Sevenoaks lines. The station gave the impetus for development, and the break-up of Birchwood Farm, the opportunity. (The station name change, from Sevenoaks to Swanley Junction after the nearest village, might better have reflected the Birchwood connection, thus avoiding confusion with the original Swanley). An ambitious scheme was envisaged for high-class villas in 'Birchwood Park'.

Meanwhile, a Royal Commission pronounced north-west Kent a healthy neighbourhood, and mental hospital, fever hospital and convalescent hospital authorities showed keen interest. In 1884 St Bartholomew's Hospital planned a convalescent home (Kettlewell), and in 1897 the Metropolitan Asylums Board, a residential school for ophthalmic children. These developments put off would-be villa buyers. South of the Rochester line terraced housing was built but, with the railway sidings holding manure trucks intended for Longfield Hill depôt, soon began to deteriorate. The Lullingstone Castle Hotel (now the Mulberry Bush) became associated with fruit and hop-pickers. However, shops, a fire station, and a jam factory, encouraged further development. The first Congregational church was built in 1890; a new one, now the United Reformed church, in 1902.

Local nurseries thrived: Cannell, Ladd and Stuart Ogg were well-known names. Cannell's slogan was 'Swanley, the home of flowers', and they exhibited at the Antwerp Exhibition in 1889.

Only 30 years after the creation of Swanley parish, the Vicar of Swanley (Rev Sir Charles Shaw, Bart) realised that Swanley Junction (as it was then called) must become a separate ecclesiastical parish. In 1900 Sir William Hart Dyke gave land for a church, and Lady Emily laid the foundation stone of St Mary's that year. The parish was created in 1901. Again the question of name arose, Swanley *Junction* naturally being disliked. The 'Birchwood Park' idea having lapsed, Rev Shaw suggested 'Swanley St Mary' to maintain separate identity for both places, but the final choice was Swanley.

In 1939 a new station was sited above the rail junction, and after World War II expansion began in earnest. A civil parish was created. The Heath estate was developed, then a council estate and comprehensive school. With a shopping centre, White Oak sports centre, and generally rapid expansion, Swanley was really under way. Even the War Memorial of 1922 was re-sited. The Memorial Hall at Five Wents, extended in 1938 and used by three communities, was first neglected, then revitalised. A by-pass, diversion of the old London road, a second shopping centre – and by 1981 Swanley's population was 20,945! Like older Swanscombe, Swanley was granted a Town Council with a Mayor.

Axstane's 1,000 year basic unity cannot be forgotten. The villages fall into three groups: Darent Valley (Wilmington to Lullingstone), Thames-side (Stone to Swanscombe), and Downland

(Fawkham to West Kingsdown), with Southfleet, Longfield, and the Swanleys not clearly in any group. But all retain individuality and present variety.

A major factor has been the break-up of many large estates. In Wilmington in 1837 the Austen estate (a family distantly related to Jane Austen) was sold, the Hall, Rowhill (and part of Joyden's Wood), Barn End, and Shire Hall, becoming separated. The general result has been to create small modern enclaves between older properties, such as the former brewery and James Bentley's laundry site, and Valley Farm (Hurfield, incorrectly called Hurlfield). The Hall has been replaced by schools, and Sir James Whitehead's Manor House and the Grange are occupied by Wilmington Girls' Grammar School.

In 1886 Lord Randolph Churchill, father of Sir Winston, made an important foreign policy speech in Oakfield Park; Sir Winston called this his father's finest speech. 19th century personalities included Rev Frederick Heberden (Vicar 1840–76) and his daughter (who died in 1940 aged 99), the two Miss Whiteheads, Miss Emily Lumb, and Edwin Deavin (80 years in the church choir!); all did much work for the village. Despite the doubling of population since 1951 to 6,955 (1981) the Wilmington Society is keen to maintain the village identity.

Darenth too has seen its important families depart, and the Grange is now an old people's home. The Southern Hospital has closed. Lane's (Lane) End saw the development of the Watchgate estate. But some recall cricketing families like the Ludlows and Hollands, who could make up complete teams on their own. Over the hill by the Church, Court Lodge (like St Margaret's) farm houses a business other than farming, but there is some revitalisation here with large new houses near the Church.

Sutton, a long main road village, still retains some ancient properties, St John's Jerusalem in particular (now in the care of the National Trust); but Sutton Place was demolished in 1968, and Cedar Lawn and the two Miss Russells have gone. Baptists, Methodists and Roman Catholics all have their small chapels.

The original Swanley, though possessing little that is really ancient, remains secluded, and its preserves factory is relevant to the agricultural aspect of the village, still largely surrounded by fields. Ewan Christian's church, St Paul's, is one of his best designs, and its broach spire sets a traditional note.

South Darenth, nudging Sutton but part of Horton Kirby, has evolved from domination by the papermill to become virtually a commuter village (always a possibility with Farningham Road Station nearby, while the motor-car has helped this phase).

Horton itself, with its many flint walls, Church and Court Lodge farm hard by, and its close-knit character between The Street and Lombard (Lumber) Street, retains some of the essence of a Downland village. In the late 19th century, Reynold's Place was home to Tom Aldworth, Dartford brewer with Richard Coomb Miller of Oakfield Lodge, Wilmington. In the churchyard lie John Banister and Tyrone Power of Franks, a forebear of the film star. Church Gates cottage was a pub. From 1793 to 1827 the village had its own workhouse, and about 1840 a sub-post office (now gone despite a population increase of four times – to 2,948 (1981).

A20 by-passed Farningham in 1922–3 and the village retains its 18th century character. In the 1830s there were steeplechases from here to Dartford. In World War II Farningham claimed to be the most bombed parish in the county, but amazingly only twelve people were injured. The population in 1981 was 1,331 – only three more than 80 years before.

Eynsford, the largest parish, is another long turnpike village, but with its double-centre origin still clear. Ford House was probably an 18th century coaching inn. Elliott Downs Till (1853–1935) inspired the first Eynsford Arbor Day (1897) when many trees were planted to enhance the village's beauty. In 1907 he adapted Little Mote, later sold to Sir Henry Fountain; Lady Fountain later bought the Castle for £50, transferring it to the Society for the Protection of Ancient Buildings. It is now in the care of the Department of Environment. Bower House was formerly the workhouse and the stocks were placed nearby in 1904. A second Baptist church was opened in 1907; a famous preacher, Spurgeon, had preached in the first one in 1852.

In 1892 James Alexander came to Home Farm; by 1980 the family farmed 2,000 acres. Business and professionals were beginning to move in (the station had opened in 1862). Solomon Cox's will (1845) left land which in 1956 made way for further development, and the Victorian vicarage was sold. Council houses had been built in Bower Lane.

E.J.Moeran, Peter Warlock and Ernest Tomlinson, composers; C.Ross Parker, writer of *There'll always be an England*; Graham Sutherland, artist, all lived in Eynsford, and Arthur Mee moved to Eynsford Hill in 1913. Percy Pilcher carried out aircraft experiments in the Austin Lodge valley in 1896.

In 1973 the benefices of Eynsford, Lullingstone and Farningham were united. Eynsford's distant hamlet, Crockenhill, retains a few flint-built cottages. In 1802 the Old Burying Ground was linked with Eynsford Baptist Church. Buried there was Edwin Vinson of High Croft Hall (1921), a large-scale strawberry grower. Crockenhill Church was opened c1852 and the Union Chapel in 1861.

At Lullingstone, after Sir William Hart Dyke's death in 1931, his son Sir Oliver inherited death duty problems. In 1934 over 5,000 acres were sold to Kemp Town Brewery Brighton Ltd. That year Lady Zöe commenced the famous Lullingstone Silk Farm, which Queen Mary visited in 1936, and where silk for the 1937 Coronation robes was spun. (The Silk Farm left in 1957 and is now near Sherborne, Dorset).

The Green Belt Act led to Kent County Council purchasing part of the Kemp Town land, but the Brewery were hopeful of providing a site for a new London airport, for which the Southern Railway built a station. World War II precluded this development and the Park then became a decoy airfield; later various Army units and Government departments occupied the Park. In 1957 the KCC granted DRDC a long lease of the Park (later transferred to Sevenoaks District Council) and in 1966 a golf-course was established.

Sir Oliver died in 1969 and, while Derek Hart Dyke inherited the title, he settled in Canada. Guy Hart Dyke remained at the Castle.

West Kingsdown has the London–Maidstone road (A20) running through its heart. This convenient artery, together with the break-up of estates, led to ribbon development between the Wars. In 1919 the Kingsdown estate (including Hever Farm) was sold; some houses were built, but many plots were used for shacks. In 1934 'Kingsdown Garden Village' was advertised on the Kingsfield Estate, based on Green Farm. This was only partly developed, and the title now seems ironic. Cafés began to spring up on the main road. Church Wood was threatened with development in 1928 but the far-sighted Rector, Canon Warland, appealed for financial assistance, and it was conveyed to the Diocese of Rochester in 1933. 61 acres were conveyed to the Forestry Commission, but this land too came under threat, and the Parish Council had to purchase it quickly. East Hill and Knatts Farms were sold in 1921–2 as smallholdings for ex-soldiers, but this led to scrappy development on poor soil. Other proposals were for a 'model village' in the Maplescombe Valley (1925), and a Knatts Valley development (1937). Threats of almost total development were real, and the magnificent view down the valley from Knockmill would have been ruined.

Brands Hatch House was originally Georgian. It was extended after 1874 by Charles Truwhitt and in 1903 seems to have been purchased by H.B.Hohler of Fawkham Manor. In 1874 Edward Pink bought Brands Hatch Farm and built Portobello (later Kingsdown) House.

But Brands Hatch is now an international name. In 1926 the Farm was bought by Henry White and in 1932 four motor-cycle clubs formed the 'Brands Hatch Combine' to organise racing. F.H.Gough bought the farm about 1936 and Harry White advertised 'Brands Hatch Pleasure Park'. New cafés and garages sprang up. World War II forestalled immediate development. In

Hollywood Manor an important RAF Intelligence Unit was installed. Many air-warfare incidents occurred over Kingsdown.

After the war, development continued, including ten sites for mobile homes. The population rose from 1,774 (1951) to 4,893 (1981).

Brands Hatch Speedway Ltd succeeded the Combine in 1949 and the first cars appeared on the track which, despite local opposition, was doubled in size in 1959-60 and the land taken over by Grovewood Securities Ltd (Eagle Star Insurance Co Ltd). The track became an alternate venue for the British Grand Prix. Despite its division by the busy A20 (relieved in 1976 by M20) the essentials of the village remain. In 1963 half the working population worked in London.

At Earlylands, probably originally a 17th century house, lived the eminent oratorio soprano, Mme Stiles-Allen, who died in 1982 at 92.

In direct contrast, Ridley remains its quiet, unsequestered self. Opposite church and farm stands Bowdler's Well, remembering Thomas Bowdler, early 19th century Rector who lost four children due to their drinking stagnant water; he was nephew of Dr Thomas Bowdler, whose literary efforts led to the term 'bowdlerise'.

Both Ridley and Ash churches suffered little from over-restoration, although Ash did have its furnishings renewed. Although there has been road-straightening at West Yoke, The Street retains several old buildings, including the Old Rectory.

It is of course at New Ash Green that modernity has come. Originally a somewhat idealistic vision of Span and Eric Lyons and Partners, the development was granted planning permission in 1964. It incorporates several neighbourhood groups, a shopping centre with mainly small shops and a pub at the end of a winding street, a school, library and welfare centre. Unfortunately the original idea lost impetus and Bovis, successors to Span, felt obliged to develop more orthodox (and less inspired) types of dwelling. The early proposals were for 5–6,000 inhabitants; the population is at present about 6,000. The ecclesiastical parish has become Ash with New Ash Green, and is based on the medieval parish church.

Hartley – by contrast again – developed in piece-meal fashion, although its more recent development has been more spaciously and pleasantly sited. A few old buildings can still be found, while All Saints church suggests Erclei's true antiquity. The tithe barn was demolished in the mid-19th century, though that used for the Roman Catholic Oratory of St Francis de Sales may also be 400 years old. About the end of the 19th century buyers were eager for land as the farming estates broke up. Colonel Joseph Hartley bought Old Downs, where he built a lodge (1882), then a house. Fairby was purchased by Small Owners Ltd, who also acquired Hartley Court. The population doubled between 1911 (278) and 1921 (568), but between 1951 and 1981 it rose from 1,255 to 6,936! Hartley Court returned to the Andrus family in 1936, but in 1952 F.Sedley Andrus inherited Scadbury (Southfleet) and the Court was sold.

Longfield has developed in nondescript fashion along its shallow valley, again a commuter development prompted by the railway. The station was erected c1870 after a request by J.B.Hohler of Fawkham Manor, and named Fawkham. In 1913 Longfield Halt on the Gravesened West line opened, but passenger services ceased in 1953. 19th century connections included Mordecai Andrus, who was farming at Longfield Hill by 1811, but later moved to Clock House, Green Street Green. Meanwhile William Benstead, who married Mary Andrus, lived at Longfield Court before moving in 1831 to Hartley Court. Mordecai died in 1838 and is buried at Longfield. About 1961 a large secondary school was opened.

Southfleet is a nucleated village, completely surrounded by arable land. In 1840 the Brooks left Hook Place to Sir John Kenwood Shaw, who took the name Brook; in 1849 it was sold to Thomas Colyer (1808–74). Thomas was born at Mates Farm, Betsham, son of another Thomas Colyer who, in 1815, built and moved to Joyce Hall, Betsham. The second Thomas's daughter married James Ferguson and their son became Sir Thomas Colyer-Ferguson (1865–1951) of Wombwell Hall,

Gravesend, and later of Ightham Mote. He transcribed many parish registers in West Kent and London.

Tenants at Hook Place were Thomas Walls, followed by the French family and John Barker (1934). In 1957 the Colyer-Fergusons sold Hook Place to J.J.Barker, who formed J.J.Barker (Southfleet) Ltd, an organisation producing a wide range of vegetables, and doing its own packaging, marketing and transportation; it also operates Hollands Farm, Hawley, and Hill Farm, Farningham. The house remains partly of the 16th and 17th centuries.

At Scadbury, after the Sedleys left, the Allens became tenants, followed by the Andrus family. Francis Bain Andrus bought Scadbury in 1890, and it was then that F.Sedley Andrus MVO MA inherited it and moved from Hartley Court. He sold the house in 1969; the farm is now leased to Stanhill Farms Ltd.

Southfleet did not escape 'Bomb Alley' danger in World War II, and the Church suffered serious damage in 1944. Since World War II, little development has taken place, but recently a discreetly infilled estate, Sedley, has been contrived near the village centre. The population in 1981 was 3,078, over twice the 1951 population; this has been largely due to the development of New Barn, a mile from the village.

Swanscombe's industrial growth brought terraced housing, several new streets, and a new church at Galley Hill, designed by Norman Shaw (of New Scotland Yard fame) and built in 1894, but never given its south aisle. All Saints Galley Hill is now closed; the town grew little further on this north side. After 1921 the population levelled at about 8,500 (1981: 8,792). For 49 years Rev G.C.Renouard was Rector. In the *Gentleman's Magazine* (April 1867) a tribute was paid to his learning. The Council offices stand on the Manor House site, and the farmhouse has unfortunately gone.

In 1820, Alderman Harman purchased Ingress Abbey and rebuilt it in magnificent style in 1833, with stone from London Bridge. The little port of Greenhithe with its new pier (1842) saw Sir John Franklin sail for the North West Passage in 1845. But the railway heralded a change to a resort and, even before it came (1849), the imposing villas of Cobham Terrace (1846) were tempting middle-class commuters. In that year a church was discussed, St Mary's was consecrated in 1856, and a parish carved out of Swanscombe and Stone. The Church, Gothic in style, is well-proportioned. Severely damaged by bombing, it was restored under Rector Rev Charles Strong MBE. Its Victorian and modern glass strongly reminds of the sea; Trevor Hayes, midshipman killed at Jutland in 1916, has both east and west windows to his memory; there is a Seamen's memorial window, and several to members of the shipbuilding Everard family. One window commemorates a son of Dr Thomas Arnold, famous headmaster of Rugby School.

A Congregational chapel was established in 1819, a Methodist chapel in 1836 in Avenue Road (transferred in 1908 to London Road), and a Roman Catholic chapel (Our Lady of Mount Carmel) was founded near the Chantry in 1863.

Middle-class social life prevailed during the mid-19th century, and the Royal Thames Yacht Club established itself here; there was fox-hunting in the hinterland too. Sam Beeton and his wife Isabella (authoress of the famous *Household Management*) settled at Mount Pleasant (Mounts Road), where in 1865 Isabella died, aged only 28. Henry Stopes settled in Greenhithe to pursue his archaeological interests, and with him was his more famous daughter, Marie.

But smoke and cement dust, and an increase in terraced housing for the working class, eventually drove most of the professional people away. Much of the terraced housing developed around Knockhall, and to serve that area, the Ingress Vale Independent Chapel was built in 1860.

In 1894–5 much excitement was generated when the Thames was frozen over. In 1909 the entire Home and Atlantic Fleets visited the Thames and the cruisers HMSs *Isis* and *Dido* anchored off Greenhithe; the village was gay with bunting and crowds greeted the crews.

But Greenhithe is also important for HMS *Worcester*. The Thames Nautical Training College was founded in 1862, and the first Training Ship of that name came to Greenhithe in 1871. The second (1877–1939) was a two-deck 86-gun warship converted to steam; and the third came in 1945. The Inner London Education Authority took over in 1968, but in 1976 the Duke of Edinburgh opened the new land-based Merchant Navy College in Ingress Abbey grounds. This incorporated the Thames Nautical Training College (HMS *Worcester*) and part of the King Edward VII Nautical College.

For many years *Worcester* was not alone; the *Warspite* and *Arethusa* were also there, and in 1938 the *Cutty Sark* was anchored off-shore, before its restoration.

With the closure of the cement works, and with Dartford Borough Council aid, Greenhithe is now undergoing rehabilitation and entering a new phase.

With the removal of much industry, Stone remains largely agricultural, particularly around Bean (now transferred ecclesiastically to Southfleet parish). Its northern area is divided between the early centre around the Parish Church (and Horn's Cross on the main London road), and the 19th century growth areas around St John's Hole, and towards the Dartford boundary. The medieval rectory still stands (a Victorian one has come and gone, demolished in 1966, like the National School nearby).

Stone Castle had various lessees, including Arthur C. Davis JP, a Lord Mayor. It is occupied by Blue Circle. Another of Axstane's worthy 19th century rectors was Canon F.W.Murray (Rector 1857–1906). He gave 50% of the costs of G.E.Street's restoration of the Church, following earlier work by Edward Cresy.

At St John's Hole was a toll-gate, east of the Welsh Tavern. There was further development in this area after World War II. A Methodist church was erected in Milestone Road (further west) in 1891. 'The City of London Lunatic Asylum' was built in 1866, the large chapel added in 1898. The City Arms was built opposite, on the main road, for the benefit of visitors; it is now used as commercial premises. The less well-known St Mary's Home was established in 1866 after transferring from Tenterden (having been founded there in 1860). It was demolished in 1961–2. Darenth Park, with its nearly half-mile frontage, was built between 1876 and 1888; it is used for the mentally defective. A noteworthy Chairman of Stone Parish Council earlier in the 20th century was Lorenzo Fuller, to whom a memorial hall was dedicated.

These then are the varied villages which have contributed to the history and variety of Axstane Hundred.

OPPOSITE: Oakfield Park, 2 October 1886; scene of Lord Randolph Churchill's 'Dartford Speech'. (KCL DD) ABOVE: Sir James Whitehead Bart, of Wilmington Manor, with Mrs Delacourt, formerly his governess, on her 100th birthday (August 1910). Her daughter is behind them. (DM/KCL DD)

ABOVE: James Bentley Ltd, *The* Laundry, Wilmington; 'Midst the Orchards of Kent' was the firm's slogan. (TS) BELOW: Wilmington Cricket Club, 1933; Dartford Heath Ground. (Note the railway carriage pavilion). (JB/ KCL DD)

ABOVE: Darenth Paper Mill. (W) CENTRE: Cottages formerly in Parsonage Lane, near Darenth bridge, 1920. (HSB/KCL DD) BELOW: Lane's (or Lane) End, Darenth early this century. (GWJ/KCL DD)

ABOVE: Hawley Manor c1910 (destroyed by fire 1919) and CENTRE: Hawley Paper Mill, c1906. (Both KCL DD) BELOW: Home of Hextable Horticultural College, facing the Limes Avenue, (house now demolished); (JB) RIGHT: Dr Kate Barrett CBE Principal, 1916–44. (JB)

ABOVE: The Cross Roads, Hextable, looking west, pre–1914. (RAG) BELOW: Salvation Army members outside Meeting Hall, Ship Lane, Sutton-at-Hone, c1890. (Third from left, back row, Mr G. Redsell, local shopowner.) (F/KCL DD)

ABOVE: Original premises of G.J.Garrett, ironmonger, Main Road, Sutton-at-Hone c1910. (Boy on left is Mr Chalcraft). (FWC/KCL DD) BELOW: Maypole Dance in Church Meadow, Swanley c1925 (Vicarage in background). (KCL DD)

ABOVE: The original Swanley Junction Station, and CENTRE: High Street, early 1900's. (Both GP) BELOW: Crockenhill church, pre–1909. (KCL DD)

HEARN.

EXE 589

OPPOSITE ABOVE: The Bridge, Farningham; from a watercolour by an unknown artist, 1875 — apart from the loss of the great chestnut tree, the view is little changed. (MJ/KCL DD) LEFT: The Hearn family's shop, Farningham, c1860. Marianne Hearn (pen-name Farningham) lived here 1834–57. (HA/KCL DD) RIGHT: The World War I tank once stood in Farningham as a monument to Major W.G.Wilson CMG of Charton Farm, who collaborated in its development. (JT.) ABOVE: An early 20th century Dartford–Farningham 'bus, manufactured by J. & E. Hall Ltd, Dartford, operated by D.F.Pitt & Sons; Mr Alfred Playle second from left, front row. (AP) BELOW: A village funeral c1900. (S-B)

ABOVE: Farningham High Street, looking east. (The post-card, dated February 1913, tells of a fox-hunt that day through Farningham Woods).
BELOW: Farningham School, class III, c1910. (Both KR)

ABOVE: Eynsford Bridge and Church c1900, though possibly earlier. LEFT: Elliott Downs Till of Eynsford, c1910. (Both KCL DD) RIGHT: Arthur Mee and his daughter, Marjorie, at Eynsford Hill c1920. (Miss Mee died in 1983). (KCL DD)

LEFT: The weathervane, Eynsford Church; Mr. E.D.Till on right, c1902. (HH) RIGHT: Sir William and Lady Emily Hart Dyke near the Gatehouse to Lullingstone Castle, c1900. (FWJ/KCL DD) BELOW: An Arnold & Foster Ltd float for the Lord Mayor's Show, 1929; demonstration of hand papermaking, with Mr Chas Rivers (young man on float). (KR)

ABOVE: West Kingsdown School, Mr Paul Palfreyman, headmaster, c1922–3. (WS) BELOW: The Street, Ash. c1905. (KCL DD)

ABOVE: Ash School, Group III, c1910. (WS) BELOW: Hartley Green and School, c1910. (DGR)

ABOVE: Longfield Hill, c1905. BELOW: Longfield (Main Road looking east at Hoselands Hill corner). (Both DGR)

ABOVE: Fawkham (now Longfield) Station, c1900. (ECY/KCL DD)
BELOW: Southfleet Stores. (SS)

ABOVE: Southfleet Scouts – early 1920s. (EHL) LEFT: Rev Wm Marcus Falloon, Rector of Southfleet 1931–53. (SF) RIGHT: Ingress Abbey as rebuilt in the 19th century. (K)

ABOVE: Swanscombe and Greenhithe Fire Brigade c1910; fireman holding horse is Mr Albert Nettleingham, a blacksmith at Greenhithe. (MMC/KCL DD) BELOW: No 4 Pit, Milton Street, Swanscombe. (KCL DD)

ABOVE: Swanscombe United FC: winners, Dartford & District League 1909 and 1910, and Gravesend Borough League 1900 and 1910. (J) CENTRE: Galley Hill Infant School class, 1928. (CT) BELOW: Greenhithe lock-up and workhouse, early this century. (WW/KCL DD)

GREENHITHE, Aug. 22nd.

A little ~~hamlet named~~ Greenhithe was known in '24,
The persons then who peopled it were numbered 'bout ~~three-score,~~
But, thanks to some with energy, who capital invested,
Now near 2000 living souls are weekly interested.

Who are those folks? John Bazley White & Bros., are their names, Sir,
In England, Scotland, Ireland and abroad, it's all the same, Sir;
They want Cement with fancy marks; they do not wish to trouble you;
They want the right-down regular thing, that's marked with J.B.W.

Now those who wish to stop the make of this must be demented,
Whilst those who wish to go a-head together are cemented.
Come Batten, Jannings, Umfreville, Vulliamy and Plunkett,
And in the Court of Chancery you soon will have to funk it.

~~The doctors are the sort of folks to~~ judge about the danger
Of living in a country place, than any Plunkett stranger.
Now Cook and Crook they both agree the place is awful healthy;
By "Hook and Crook" they rub along, but never can be wealthy.

Then at Greenhithe there are some ships, in fact they're not a few, Sir,
There's the "Worcester" & the "Chichester" & the "Saucy Arethusa."
Ask Captain Smith, or Thorburn too, I'll guarantee their answer;
They have'nt got a *boy* unwell, nor yet a single *man*, Sir.

Then why this stupid, senseless fuss, this blessed tommy-fooley?
Which reminds you of the tailors nine, who lived in street call'd Tooley
Who fancied they were England all. Ah! they were thoughtless Asses.
Some folks', who dwell at Greenhithe now, their folly much surpasses.

Then Hurrah! my brave boys, ~~you will never repent,~~
If you stick to your work and stand up for Cement,
The moral to draw is, beyond all the others:
Stand fast by the firm of J. B. White & Brothers.

ANTI-PLUNKETT.

A rhyming attack on opponents of the cement industry in the Swanscombe–Greenhithe area. (KCL DD)

ABOVE: St Mary's Church, Greenhithe; consecrated 1856. (From a contemporary drawing) BELOW: Ice on the Thames, 1895; HMS *Worcester* off-shore. (Both KCL DD)

ABOVE: High Street, Greenhithe, c1910. BELOW: Captain Scott's ship *Terra Nova* off Greenhithe, 1 June 1910, soon to leave for Antarctica for the last time. (Both KCL, DD)

ABOVE: From right to left: HMS *Worcester*, the clipper *Cutty Sark*, and the grain-shiip *Penang*, off Greenhithe, 17 January 1939. (EGB/KCL DD)
BELOW: London Road, Stone (St John's Hole); old toll house in foreground, left. (KCL DD)

LEFT: Tram at Horn's Cross terminus c1910. RIGHT: Tommy Peerless at Littlebrook Farm c1910. BELOW: Stone Parish Council February, 1928. (All KCL DD)

ABOVE: Former Dame School building, Horton Kirby, c1900. (KCL DD)
BELOW: River Darent near Franks Hall, Horton Kirby. (KCL DD)

ABOVE: Centenary of Horton Kirby CE South Primary School, 1957; teacher in charge: Mrs Evans. (MG) BELOW: Axstane.

A Crystal Ball

'Your guess is as good as mine' – no doubt at all!

Few of us can be absolutely sure of future developments. Plans made with one intention frequently have unforeseen consequences, if only because people have their own ideas. New inventions too bring new ideas, ideas bring new theories, some even bring new philosophies. I have written earlier 'There are no eternal hills' and, although there may be eternal truths, they allow of much flexibility without damage to their essence.

Of one thing we may be sure; there will be change. With London so close, how could it be otherwise? The building of M25 has suggested a city encirclement not so much limiting expansion as encouraging development to that perimeter; since M25 cuts through Axstane there is clearly concern here. Industry, housing, roads, are all likely to intertwine their pressures on western Axstane. Nevertheless, though Axstane produces wheat, man still does not live by bread alone (which was one realisation behind the Green Belt Act of 1938). Thus, while one may say there are new theories arguing against a Green Belt policy, another may counter-argue that that policy was linked (if only subconsciously) with an eternal truth which should not be disregarded. Flexibility and understanding will thus be required. The most likely outcome may be compromise.

One ultimate question is 'Shall Dartford – and western Axstane – become part of administrative London?' After all, towns further west have been swallowed – why not this district? One foresees fierce argument for, whatever diagrams and maps may suggest, the human element remains, and its judgment must dominate the situation, not the reverse.

So far as one can see ahead, the need for agriculture in Axstane will not subside. Man may indeed not live by bread *alone*, but he still needs bread. The improved efficiency of Axstane's farmers – and how many there are! – suggests a continued thriving of this essential industry (for industry it is).

Certainly, however, there will be more leisure, suggesting perhaps more 'leisure centres', though one hopes that 'leisure' will also lead to a greater appreciation of the land and countryside, of which Axstane still has much to offer.

More infilling of villages with new housing, more schools (with suggestions for using school land for other purposes during vacations), more old people's homes and facilities, more community schemes – all will require more, not less, planning. But planning itself is evolving, itself under pressure to meet varied needs – including proponents and opponents of particular developments. *In the long run* it will do what most require, whoever the 'most' are who do their homework thoroughly and put their case clearly and effectively.

I foresee Axstane surviving the pressures because of a greater general and local awareness of what is often loosely called 'the environment'. It will not be an easy passage but here, beside the Dartford Tunnel, one dares to take the sanguine view.

Bibliography

General
Archaeologia Cantiana (Kent Archaeological Society), various volumes.
Banister, J.: *A Synopsis of Husbandry*, (1799).
Chalklin, C.W.: *Seventeenth Century Kent* (John Hallewell Publications, 1965).
Dewey, H. etc.: *Geology of the Country around Dartford* (HMSO, 1924) (and related vols of the British Regional Geology series).
Everitt, A.: *The Community of Kent and the Great Rebellion, 1640–60* (Leicester University Press, 1966).
Francis, A.J.: *The Cement Industry 1796–1914* (David and Charles, 1977).
Freeman, Sarah: *Isabella and Sam* (V. Gollancz, 1977).
Hasted, Edward: *The History and Topographical Survey of Kent* (2nd edn. 1797–1801).
Hoskins, W.G.: *Fieldwork in Local History* (Faber and Faber, 1982).
Jessup, Frank W.: *A History of Kent* (Phillimore, 1974).
Lambarde, William: *A Perambulation of Kent* (1576).
Melling, Elizabeth : (Ed.) *Kentish Sources* Series I–VI (KCC, 1959–69).
Morgan, Philip: (Ed.) *Domesday Book (Kent)* (Phillimore, 1983).
Newman, John: *West Kent and the Weald (Buildings of England* Series), Nikolaus Pevsner (Ed.) (Penguin, 1969).
Oddy and Miller: *Making of the Modern British Diet:* (Agricultural Labourer's Standard of Living in Kent 1790–1840) (Crown Helm).
Pallant, N.: *The Gravesend West Branch* (Oakwood Press, 1984).
Philip, B. J.: *Archaeological Excavations in the Darent Valley*. (CIB Archaeological Rescue Corps, 1973).
Rogers, Philip: *A Vale in Kent* (P.M.E. Erwood Publications Ltd 1955).
Shorter: *Papermills in England 1495–1800* (Vol VI).
Thorpe, John, MD, FRS· *Registrum Roffense* (1769).
Thorpe, John, MA, FSA: *Custumale Roffense* (1788).
Victoria County History (Vols I and III).
Waechter, J: *Man before History* (Elsevier–Phaidon, 1976) (especially for Swanscombe Man).
Wallenburg, J.K.: *Kentish Place Names* (1931) (Uppsala) *Place Names of Kent* (1934) (Uppsala).
Witney, K. P.: *The Jutish Forest* (Univ. of London, 1976).

Villages
Ash, A History of (Typescript) (W. Frank Proudfoot).
Eynsford, A History of (H.H. Bassett) (c1910).
Eynsford (W.I. Curnow) (1980 edn).
Eynsford, A study of the Parish (E.R. Kidd) (1965).
Fawkham: The Story of a Kentish Village (W. Frank Proudfoot).
Greenhithe, A short history of (W. Tovey) (1962).
Hartley through the ages (G.W. Bancks) (1927).
Lullingstone Park (Susan Pittman) (Meresborough Books, 1983).
South Darenth: The growth and Decline of an Industrial Village (Malcolm Green) (1974).
Stone: A study of the Parish of (Jacqueline Carter) (1969).
Swanscombe through the Ages (F.L. Ralph) (1964).
Swanscombe, A history of (J. Sparvel-Bayly, FSA) (1875).
Special studies:.
The old Burying Ground, Crockenhill.)
Farningham Crossroads.) (Shirley Burgoyne Black) (Darent Valley Publications 1981–4)
Children of Farningham and their Schools.)
Church guide books (various authors, but particularly those of H.J. Balls, which include *Sutton-at-Hone Church and its Worshippers* which brings the church in closer relationship with the village).

Other material consulted included :.
Census Returns 1801–1981.
Dartford Central Library Local History Collection.
Dartford Historical and Antiquarian Society "Transactions" and annual "*News-letters*".
Dunkin, A.J. Scrapbooks.(Kent County Library, Springfield,Maidstone).
Kent County Archives Office: Tithe Awards and Maps for each parish, Vestry Minutes, and other catalogued material.
Kentish Times (Various issues, but particularly 1930s series of articles on villages by Norris Willatt).
Miller, R. C. MS annual Diaries, 1873–1887.
Rochester Diocesan Directories.

Much material concerning the manorial and other estates came from the MS papers of the late Horace John Balls held by Dartford Central Library; knowing him personally as I did, I am sure that he would be pleased to know that much of his hitherto unpublished material has at last been used.

Key to Caption Credits

AC	Alfred Cumberland
AP	Alfred Playle
BL	British Library
BM (Nat Hist)	British Museum (Natural History)
CEF	C.E.Francis
CT	Mrs. C.Thompson
CY	Clement Youens
DDAG	Dartford District Archaeological Group
DGR	Douglas Grierson
DH	Derek Hicks
DM	*Daily Mirror*
ECY	E.C.Youens
ED	Miss E.L.Duff
EGB	E.G.Brand
EHL	E.H.Lane
F	Miss Fairey
FWC	F.W.Chalcraft
FWJ	F.W.Judge
GG	G.Gates
GWJ	G.W.Judge
GP	Mrs. G.Puplett
H	Edward Hasted
HA	Mrs H.Atfield
HH	Mrs Hilary Harding
HJB	H.J.Balls
HSB	H.S.Bewger
J	Mr. Jarman
JB	Mrs. Jean Boon
JT	John Topham
K	Mrs B.Knott
KCAO	Kent County Archives Office
KCL DD	Kent County Library (Dartford Division)
KR	Mrs. K.Rivers
KT	*The Kentish Times*
MC	Mavis Chattenton
MG	Malcolm Green
MJ	Mike Jesson
MMC	Mrs. M.M.Curry
PF	Peter Flewin
PRO	Public Record Office
RAG	R.A.Graham
RH	Reg. Hollick
RW	Roger Walsh
S-B	Mr. Sheridan-Boulton
SF	S.Falloon
SS	Southfleet School
TS	Terry Sims
W	Mrs. Ward
WS	Mrs. Wilkins
WW	W.Whiffin

Index

Figures in italics refer to illustrations

Subscribers

Presentation Copies

1 Dartford Borough Council
2 Sevenoaks District Council
3 Kent County Council
4 Dartford Library
5 Dartford Borough Museum
6 John Newman

7 Geoff Porteus
8 Clive & Carolyn Birch
9 Michael Jesson
10 W.E.M.Arundell
11 Geoff Beetles
12 Miss P.M.Stevens
13 Mr & Mrs E.S.Good
14 Mr & Mrs B.V.Wiffen
15 Beryl & Derrick Taylor
16 Miss A.Anders
17 Mrs M.Gardiner
18 Mr & Mrs T.A.Jarman
19 Mrs D.J.Honnor
20 Ken Jarvis
21 Mrs S.E.Napier
22 Miss D.M.Cannell
23 Mrs P.Carey
24 J.M.Morgan
25 Mrs A.E.Watkins
26 Dartford Borough Museum
27 C.R.Baker
28 Dartford District Archaeological Group
29 Mrs Margaret Giddings
30
31 Mr & Mrs J.L.Topping
32 Dr H.D.Cheetham
33 Doris & Alfred Larratt
34 Mrs Zoe Walker
35 Alan Frederick Robinson
36 Miss J.Shepherd
37 Mr & Mrs A.P.Conroy
38 P.W.Boreham
39 Victoria & Albert Museum
40 London Guildhall Library
41 Gerald Cramp
42 K.Cousins
43 Mr & Mrs L.A.Taylor
44 Mr & Mrs D.J.C. Simpson
45 F.H.Hyate
46 Andrew D.Pomfret
47 James H. & Alexander Britton
48 Jeannette M.H.Carter
49 R.A.Knott
50 Gordon & Penny Martin
51 J.L.Hutchinson
52 Mr & Mrs W.G.Ford
53 Mr & Mrs T.Cook
54 Paul Snoswell
55 David E.A.Chapman
56 Mrs B.W.Winfield
57 Mrs B.M.Gray
58 Miss T.Cooper
59 M.McGuinness
60 Mrs D.M.Owen
61 Mrs B.J.Simmons
62 Mrs Doris M.Moore
63 Herbert J.W.Ticehurst
64 Mr & Mrs R.G.Wells
65 A.R.Garwood
66 Mr & Mrs D.C.Phillips
67 Mr & Mrs E. Banks
68 W.T.Farmer JP
69 B.C.King
70 Mrs E.A.Jenkins
71 Ian J.W.Reid
72 C.E.Morris
73 Herbert & Phyllis Jarvis
74 S.W.Allport
75 Ken Godwin
76 Martin J.S.Smith
77 Philip Treveil
78 Vanessa M.Carter
79 Mr & Mrs G.J.Spencer
80 Valerie & Ivan Crane
81 Mrs P.P.M.Hudson
82 Bryan D.F.Clarke
83 Mrs J.B.Murphy
84 F.J.White
85 P.J.Carter
86 Mr & Mrs W.G.Harley
87 Colin P.Allsop
88 Daphne M.Roberts
89 Moira A.Chandler
90 Denis Marrington
91 P.McLean
92 Mr & Mrs R.Aish
93 Norman F.Hall
94 Stuart L.Hall
95 R.Fordred
96 Mrs Beryl Gooding
97 S.J.Cook
98 Miss S.M.Morgan
99 Mrs R.L.Smith
100 Mrs Winifred Grimmette
101 J.D.Webster
102 George Ballard
103 Miss D.Wells
104 Mr & Mrs R.S.Wells
105 Mrs D.Dolden
106 James Finan
107 F.J.Turnbull
108 Judith & Peter Foreman
109 Mr & Mrs C.R.Stanyon
110 Miss N.M.Huckle
111 C.B.Jones
112 Mrs J.Taylor
113 Mrs J.Winch
114 N.L.Kemp
115 M.D.Waterman
116 Mr & Mrs R.Whymark
117 Kelvin J.Marsh
118 Trevor W.Betts
119 Mrs Trudy Mills
120 Miss M.Long
121 Mrs S.M.Cant
122 Peter Chattenton
123 Joyce E.Parker
124 Mrs Frances Gray
125 Miss B.Leach
126 Marjorie Miller
127 Mr & Mrs P.R.Storr
128 Charles & Marion Heather
129 Suzanne Beadle
130 G.E.Bignall
131 Michael Hutton
132 Miss F.R.Reeve
133 Peter Onley
134 Mrs C.M.Woodyer
135 M.V.Sawyer
136 T.H.Morgan
137 Mrs D.Green
138 Mrs Gillian Neville
139 Mrs Kerry Hawkins
140 Miss Margaret R. Pluckrose
141 Mrs Nora Shorter
142 Mr & Mrs C.Cock
143 J.H.C.Seager
144 Mr & Mrs P.W.Stone
145 R.G.Denton
146 H.C.Potterton
147 G.Bufford
148 Miss England
149 Ian C.Hammerton
150 Mrs C.Owen
151 A.W.Camp
152 E.J.Millen
153 R.T.Balcombe
154 G.A.N.Robinson
155 Mary A.Dalzell
156 Janet S.Dalzell
157 S.J.Stringer
158 Gwen & Brian Titmarsh
159 S.W.Taylor
160 Mrs S.Easter
161 Ian Marshall
162 R.Collier
163 R.J.King
164 C.Prior
165 Miss E.Martin
166 G.Bocutt
167 Mr & Mrs E.F. Churchward
168 Joyce Green Hospital Patients' Library
169 West Hill Hospital Library
170 Mr & Mrs W.T.Dann
171 Mr & Mrs L.Upsher
172 C.Benson
173 Mrs Joan P.A.Kelly
174 S.J.Stringer

175 M.Wotton
176 R.E.Good
177 Edna M.Brown
178 Miss F.Allchin
179 D.A.Baldwin
180 Mr & Mrs M.L.Carter
181 Mr & Mrs C.A.Ovenden
182 D.G.Hunt
183 Miss J.Igglesden
184 Mrs M.Brown
185 P.J. & K.L.Sargeant
186 Mrs P.M.Wray
187 T.P.Jacob
188 Mr & Mrs E.P.Seabrook-Smith
189 Mrs C.S.Cooper
190 Mrs R.M.Frost
191 Nada Hammond
192 G.S.Hudson-Peacock
193 Mrs A.Powell
194 Geoff H.Porteus
195 Mrs L.Clifford
196 C.A.Willeard
197 Mr & Mrs A.F.Pyefinch
198 B.J.Faint
199 J.MacDonald
200 D.Gillham
201 John B.Gilbert
202 L.A.Wakerly
203 Miss I.Morris
204 Mr & Mrs H.Phillips
205 D.S.Jewiss
206 M.D.Charman
207 Mrs M.Warby
208 J.A.Tyler
209 A.J.Tyler
210 Mary M.Moore
211 Lily M.F.Berrecloth
212 T.Berrecloth
213 Mrs D.May
214 Mrs B.J.Smith
215 E.V.Heath
216 Mr & Mrs D.J.Dodds
217 Miss B.Widocks
218 Mrs D.Phillips
219 Mr & Mrs A.Playle
220 Frank Sayers
221 Mrs Mollie Bennett
222 Mrs G.Z.Shuter
223 A.G.Macrow
224 F.M.Skone
225 Dartford Grammar
226 School
227 D.J.Patterson
228 Roy E.Hampton
229 R.H.Saunders
230 Gordon J.Young
231 Mrs B.G.Port
232 C.G.Young
233 Mr & Mrs P.F.Coleman
234 Gwen & Malcolm Rees
235 W.H.Freeman
236 Mrs M.Bridgland
237 Mr & Mrs P.G.Fricker
238 Ms L.Conyard
239 J.E.Wadey
240 Brian Playle
241 R.A.Holdstock
242 Mrs K.D.P.Norman
243 W.F.Wood
244 Mrs S.Longstaff
245 J.P.Humphrey
246 Mrs Mary Skelton
247 Neil R.Langridge
248 S. de Winton
249 Dr J.A.Reader
250 Mr & Mrs C.M.Hewett
251 Mrs Dorothy Gladwyn
252 Mrs Elizabeth Hills
253 Allan Pennell
254 M.A.Bossley
255 L.G.Blackwell
256 W.A.Bates
257 Mrs W.I.Martin
258 Peter E.Hodgkinson
259 Mr & Mrs A.Boyling
260
287 Dartford Library
288 Mr & Mrs R.D.Force
289 A.K.Pither
290 Y. & M.Pither
291 H. & K.Marshall
292 Terence Moyle
293 Mrs S.M.Supple
294 Mr & Mrs M.S.Renno
295 Mrs Margaret Vick
296 Mrs M.J.Lucking
297 Miss Margery Wadhams
298 Muriel Webster
299 D. & M.K.Gough
300 Mrs Joan C.Thomas
301 Karen & John Downes
302 Paul & Gillian Townsend
303 Bernard & Patricia Crossley
304 Robert A.Frampton
305 Mrs Mavis Chattenton
306 Mr & Mrs E.J.Smith
307 Mr & Mrs G.Mitchell
308 Mrs H.Everest
309 John W.Kemp
310 Adrian Herbert
311 A.Herbert
312 Mrs P.Drew
313 D.M.Edmunds
314 Audrey Phillips
315 Mrs S.Claydon
316
317 Mrs M.E.Jowett
318 Mr & Mrs T.Scarth
319 Peter Barber
320 Melissa Downes
321 Jonathon Downes
322 A.J.Mills
323 Mr & Mrs G.Rowell
324 Miss K.M.Goodridge
325 Janet M.Rose
326 Mrs Alice Stainer
327 Mrs D.Blades
328 Mr & Mrs R.Wells
329 Mr & Mrs J.E.White
330 G.T.Port
331 K.A.Tisdell
332 R.W. & Mrs H.Tucker
333 Mrs A.Murgatroyd
334 W.G.Williams
335 D.E.Gabb
336 D.E.Ryner
337 B.T.Hills
338 Mr & Mrs P & Usa Holmes
339 Miss Angela M.L.Barber
340 Mrs M.D.Frost
341 Mrs Sheila Hawes
342 Mr & Mrs G.Cox
343 P.Loft
344 Mr & Mrs F.W. Matthews
345 Norman Stuttle
346 R.F.Atwood
347 K.Bennett
348 M.L.Carter
349 R.J.Barnes
350 Mrs B.J.Smith
351 Mrs S.M.Darby
352 D.V.Samson
353 J.F.D.Hubert
354 Rev L.Laker
355 Roy & Kerry Hawkins
356 E.H.Walls
357 J.M.Heathfield
358 Michael Bell
359 Harold G.Reader
360 Mrs Maureen Hall
361 John Heighway
362 Mr & Mrs D.Freeman
363 A.R.Watson
364 Mick Mills
365 Roy A.Edwards
366 Mrs M.Jay
367 R.M.Pain
368 C.Fowler
369 S.M.Powis
370 G.M.Welch
371 Mrs L.J.Cooper
372 Mr & Mrs A.Neighbour
373 R.J.Paice
374 Mrs G.J.Palmer
375 James McQuillan
376 G.H.Wells
377 Mrs K.L.Sargeant
378 D.G.Parsons
379 Joyce M.Jones
380 Miss K.Berry
381 C.McKewan
382 Mrs M.Newton
383 Mr & Mrs S.Johnson
384 Ian C.Hammerton
385 Mr & Mrs Yaxley
386 G.E.F.Quincey
387 A.J.Helland
388 Mr & Mrs R.Lane
389 Dominic Kelly
390 G.F.Farr
391 Brian Luck
392 Ian M.Gould
393 Mr & Mrs A.H.Griffiths
394 C.F.Nokes
395
404 Dartford Central Library
405
406 Mrs Sheila M.Hunt
407 Mrs Nina M.Smith
408 F.J.Ashby
409 Derek Blew
410 M.A.Brown
411 Miss Alison Cook
412 B.J.Akers
413 P.F.Hulse
414 D.J.Hoare
415 A.E.Hendry
416 Mrs S.Mulheran
417 Brian Barnden
418 Paul Homer
419 Dr David King
420 Mrs M.Jackson
421 Hilary Graham
422 Lynn Burchell
423 V.R.Jarrett
424 G.P.Jarrett
425 M.R.Shillabeer
426 P.F.Horwood
427 George V.Allan
428 Trevor J.Allan
429 M.J.Medlen
430 Miss F.Bull
431 Gerald Whiting
432 J.Turner
433 Mrs Joy Linsdell
434 Mrs Pat Paice
435 Mrs J.Harling
436 Freda Skone
437 Peter G.Smith
438 H.Jarmans
439 Mrs E.C.Smith
440 Frank Warren
441 B.Danton
442 Derek Hicky
443 Mr & Mrs B.A.Hall
444 Miss Frances Armour
445 Miss B.Shaw
446 G.H.Everest
447 L.A.E.Buckingham
448 K.T.Chamberlain
449 Henry Fenton
450 B.M.Gould
451 A.Cappleman
452 Mrs S.East
453 Ken Russell
454 Philip C.Letchford
455 William Ward
456 Kevin Nash
457 Duncan Aldridge
458 Mrs P.Banks
459 Mrs P.Hawkins
460 Mrs E.Hollands
461 A.C.Denton
462 Derek Thorogood
463 Martin Smith

464 K.F.Binskin
465 Simon Price
466 Mrs B.Smith
467 Derek Hicks
468 Mrs G.Connolly
469 Mrs F.K.Riners
470 Harry R.Lambert
471 Mrs Joanne Trimmings
472 Mrs Prescott
473 A.E.Farmer
474 Terence Sims
475 Mrs & Mrs Yvonne & Colin Murphy
476 Miss E.Hyland
477 C.G.Lane
478 Betty Joan Riddell
479 Philip Matthew
480 K.Bennett
481 W.N.Guthrie
482 Mrs F.Biggs
483 Mrs C.Smith
484 M.W.Hogan
485 B.A.Phillimore
486 A.H.Blackburn
487 Mrs C.A.Bennett
488 Mr & Mrs D.J.Atkins
489 Miss M.G.Freed
490 Dartford Girls' Grammer School
491 Mrs Rita Bowler
492 Margaret Parry
493 Mrs J.Gaymer
494 Margaret Mitchell
495 G.J.McAdie
496 Alan Eadie
497 E.V.Heath
498 Mr & Mrs D.Boon
499 David & Julia Phillips
500 Roger P.Lee
501 Mrs D.R.Meddemmen
502 Brian Brockie
503 Lena Hopkins
504 David Bonnage
505 Mrs V.Baker
506 Mrs M.Downs
507 Bryan Law
508 A.C.Dellow
509 T.A.Thompson
510 Mrs E.Dunmal
511 Mrs T.Orpin
512 J.Barber
513 H.Micklethwaite
514 Mrs D.M.Shakespeare
515 A.E.Goldsmith
516 Mrs Joyce Helen Gray
517 Mrs Muriel Roebuck
518 Mrs Rose Gillies
519 Reginald W.Hollick
520 John Kierans
521 Maxwell Robert French
522 C.Maytum
523 Mrs E.Bradshaw
524 A.H.Archer
525 Robert Sacheverell Byrne

526 G.Letchford
527 Mrs S.Clark
528 P.F.W.Rose
529 R.H.C.Brown
530 Mrs M.Sayer
531 Mrs P.Bourne
532 Mrs O.Sparks
533 J.W.Robinson
534 S.G.Willson
535 Nicholas Bourne
536 P.F.Winton
537 A.C.Saunders
538 Mr & Mrs R.H.Mayne
539 G.L.Lawrence
540 Helen E.West
541 I.D.Wright
542 J.W.Channell
543 Ronin O'Connell
544 D.L.Rowland
545 C.B.Cooper
546 Mrs M.J.McKeever
547 Mrs J.Child
548 Philip Roy McGarvey
549 R.H.Turnace
550 D.R.Cracknell
551 Mrs I.Young
552 Mrs T.Heddle
553 J.Naylor
554 Miss J.L.Sands
555 Miss M.C.McDonald
556 Walter Ollerhead
557 Mrs E.L.Sparshott
558 Mrs S.Pittman
559 Miss P.P.Lewis
560 Mrs B.D.Lawrence
561 J.O.Mullen
562 Mrs V.Brown
563 Christopher David Miller
564 Mrs D.Joannou
565 Mrs P.Finch
566 Mrs B.Shead
567 Mrs T.Stevens
568 J.M.Wright
569 Mrs J.S.Taylor
570 James Mythen
571 M.J.West
572 F.Grant
573 F.J.Paell
574 Miss E.M.Lane
575 David Pearson
576 Frederick Pearson
577 Gordon Wheeler
578 Mrs G.Puplett
579 W.G.Duncombe
580 Mr & Mrs P.E. Parmenter
581 Swanley Branch, Kent
583 County Library
584 Mr & Mrs C.Crook
585 C.R.Bull
586
591 Kent County Library
592 Michael Robert Thompson

593
594 Miss E.J.Barnes
595 A.J.Barnes
596 E.G.Lane
597 Mrs D.S.Burgess
598 Mrs C.M.Edwards
599 B.Lister
600 Martin Gedney
601 Alistair Ellis
602 Mr & Mrs W.D. Lovegrove
603 Miss G.E.Crowhurst
604 Miss J.Scoones
605 Paul Carrick
606 Mrs J.G.Ley
607 Mrs Joan Baxter
608 Roy Burnett
609 D.S.Jewiss
610 M.R.Thompson
611 Rosemary Poremer
612 Peter Singleton
613 Mrs Kathleen M.Rolfe
614 R.T.W.Atkins
615 D.W.Grierson
616 Barbara J.Wake
617 Mrs A.A.Loftus
618 Shirley Orr
619 Mr & Mrs D. Hollingworth
620 Mrs N.E.Perl
621 A.H.C.Watts
622 Mrs L.Deverson
623 S.Stuart
624 Mrs S.J.Stillwell
625 B.P.Heselden
626 P.F.R.Masson
627 J.C.Evans
628 D.White
629 Mrs J.A.Brazier
630 I.Norman
631 Mrs P.Northover
632 Paulette Keenan
633 Kate Louise Davis
634 Sally Flack
635 Mr & Mrs G.H.G.Lewis
636 Mrs A.Spratley
637 Sandra Abrams
638 Geoffrey R.Ash
639 John Dunn
640 Mrs A.Atkinson
641 D.W.Walden
642 C.I.Clark
643 Mrs C.J.Clayton
644 Mrs D.Burgoyne
645 Mrs J.Underwood
646 R.F.Linklater
647 Roger Bickerstaffe
648 P.F.Baker
649 Dartford Historical & Antiquarian Society
650 Wilmington Parish
657 Council
658 Philip Lane
659 Mr & Mrs D.L.Page
660 Ian D.Armitt

661 Miss E.M.Vinall
662 Rev K.S. & Mrs B.G. Sargeant
663 Mr & Mrs D.E.Clare
664 George Pursey
665 G.Forsyth
666 Charles Fowler
667 Roy Turley
668 Marjorie Farley
669
670 Malcolm Green
671 Mr & Mrs J.C.Strachan
672 K.H.Saunderson
673 H.J.Hadlow
674 T.K.M.Beckett
675 J.S.Cope
676 Sidney Watts
677
678 Catherine R.Ross
679 Mrs H.Eden
680 Valentine Audrey Jolley
681 B.E. & P.M.Cass
682 Mrs B.Swinthinbank
683 B.W.Garner
684 Margaret E.Rose
685 Mrs Jacqueline Dawn Eden
686
687 R.White
688 Miss J.M.Aldery
689 Mrs T.J.Atfield
690 H.Rivers
691 Kenneth Leadbeater
692 James S.Oddy
693
694 Mrs B.A.Bully
695 Margaret Acton
696 T.Ludlow
697 Mrs Leonora Collins
698 R.J.Fish
699 Gladys Pile
700 R.G.R.Hogben
701 E.M.Murray
702 Margaret Maw
703 Eric C.G.Ovendale
704 E.M.Herbert
705 John Cook
706
707 Mrs.F.Cooke
708
709 D.E.Walker
710 W.J.Lowles
711 K.T.Ray
712 A.Andrew Gibbs
713 George L.Bailey
714 B.Payne
715 J.W.Bailey
716 W.F.Proudfoot
717 M.Warren
718 Jean Armour
719 M.H.Bell
720 Mrs W.Grimmette
721 H.M.Mitchell
722 Mrs M.A.Austen
723 F.L.Gardner

724 D.E.C.Hood
725 D.Porter
726 D.Dray
727 A.Bowles
728 J.M.Masters MA
729 Mrs J.Wise
730 Jean Doris Griffiths
731 Malcolm Munn
732 Mrs Gwen Phillips
733 Pamela Mercer
734 Cllr Ivor Jones
735 Janet Hawney
736 V.Sutton
737 John D.J.Baker
738 M.A.Nothard
739 Peggy Lucille Bines
740 D.C.Eades
741 Mrs D.M.Harper
742 Kathleen Beater
743 E.P.Lambert
744 Christopher Proudfoot
745 Dr Janet B.Hyde
746 Paul Tiney
747 Brian Cope
748 Joan K.E.Chalcraft
749 Francis F.Tate
750 John E.Purple
751 David W.Andrews
752 Patricia M.Jacobs

Remaining names unlisted

ENDPAPERS: FRONT – Map of Axstane Hundred in 1778, reproduced from Hasted's *History of Kent*. (KCL DD) BACK – Court Lodge Farm and Church, Southfleet; a typical medieval relationship. (DH)